D0871824

On Lenin

ON LENIN

NOTES TOWARDS A BIOGRAPHY

LEON TROTSKY

translated and annotated by Tamara Deutscher

with an introduction by Lionel Kochan

GEORGE G. HARRAP & CO. LTD
London   Toronto   Wellington   Sydney

This edition published in Great Britain 1971
by GEORGE G. HARRAP & Co LTD
182–184 High Holborn, London, W.C.1

ISBN 0 245 50301 3 (hardback)
0 245 50302 1 (paperback)

Set in Granjon type and printed by
Western Printing Services Ltd, Bristol
Made in Great Britain

Contents

Introduction

Lionel Kochan

NOT FOR nothing was the young Trotsky known as the Pen. His published work embraces a wide variety of genres—polemical writings, pamphlets, literary criticism, political theory, autobiography, biography, history, and journalism. Each piece of writing bears the unchallengable imprint of its author—and also of its time. It is for this reason that Trotsky's work must be seen in the context of his life.

He was born in 1879 in a village in the Ukraine, the son of a Jewish family of independent small farmers. After school in Odessa and Nikolayev he rapidly entered the Marxist wing of the revolutionary movement. Arrest and exile to Siberia soon followed. He escaped from Siberia in 1902 and the next year made his first contact with Lenin, Trotsky's senior by nine years. But the initial harmony (described below) was soon disrupted by their differences over the character of party organization that became manifest at the London Conference (1903). Trotsky, at this time, tended rather to align himself with the looser Menshevik view. The abortive revolution of 1905, when Trotsky became the last president of the St Petersburg Soviet, saw a further development in his views. Fortified by his experience in 1905 and in co-operation with Alexander Helphand (Parvus) he became an adherent and exponent of the theory of 'permanent revolution' which represented an attempt to adapt to the conditions of backward Russia the classical Marxist schema. But not until 1917 did the opportunity arise to put these views into practice. Trotsky passed the intervening years partly in prison but mainly in exile—

Berlin, Vienna, Paris, and New York. During this period his polemics with Lenin and the Bolsheviks continued unabated. They did not cease until the joint revolutionary fervour of both men brought them together in the spring and summer of 1917. All former disputes were buried. Thenceforward Trotsky's rise was rapid, as Lenin's closest worker. To this period he devotes the bulk of the present work. He played the chief role in the organization of the Petrograd insurrection and became successively foreign minister (commissar) of the infant Soviet regime, founder of the Red Army, and its leader in the civil war. But from 1923 onwards Trotsky's individualist destiny took a downward turn. He does not seem to have made any great effort to attend Lenin's funeral in January 1924. Both at home and abroad, Trotsky found himself increasingly isolated in an unfavourable domestic and foreign situation, a situation exploited unremittingly by Stalin and his associates. In 1925 he was removed as nominal head of the Red Army and a little later condemned by the Central Committee; in 1926 he was removed from the Politburo; in 1927 he was expelled from the Party; in 1928 exiled to Central Asia; and in 1929 expelled from Russia. He was killed on Stalin's order in 1940.

Towards the beginning of his *Philosophy of History* Hegel has a passage that describes the work of the 'elemental historian', men such as Herodotus, Thucydides, Guicciardini. "Their essential material is what is present and living in their environment," Hegel writes. "The formation of the author and that of events from which he makes his work, the spirit of the author and the spirit of the actions of which he tells *are one and the same.* He describes what he himself has more or less taken part in or at least lived through. He is not concerned with reflections, for he lives in the spirit of the matter and is not yet beyond it; if he even belongs, as does Caesar, to the class of military leaders or statesmen, then it is precisely *his aims* that are presented as history."

This passage by no means encompasses Trotsky's total magnitude as a historian, though it does indeed point to one on its characteristic features. Trotsky's *History of the Russian Revolution* remains one of the great historical achievements of all time. Its verve, analytical thrust, sheer enthusiasm, compelling narrative, mastery of complex material, and stylistic command are overwhelming in their total impact. Here the justice of Hegel's emphasis on the historian-statesman or the historian-general who identifies his aims with his history is at once apparent. Trotsky is indeed such an 'elemental historian'. Given the subsequent fate of the revolution, Trotsky's work is a triumphant vindication of Gautier's dictum:

> Tout passe.—L'Art robuste
> Seul a l'éternité;
> Le buste
> Survit à la cité.
>
> Et la médaille austère
> Que trouve un laboureur
> Sous terre
> Révèle un empereur.

Trotsky published his *History* in 1930. Since then, of course, the amount of material and documentation of all sorts has grown immeasurably. It is also true that it is difficult to use the presuppositions of Marxism—mitigated though these may be by the theory of 'permanent revolution' —as an explanatory framework for events in Russia. Again, Trotsky's work suffers from an undue concentration on events in Petrograd. No matter—for all that, his work is a rare achievement. So much, indeed, is this the case, that it still casts on the historiography of the revolution an ineffaceable shadow. Its nearest rival is perhaps Paul Milyukov's *History of The Second Russian Revolution*. This too is the work of a deeply committed partisan, a work steeped in political passion—perhaps more so even than Trotsky's, since Milyukov wrote on the very morrow of defeat and not in the calmer contemplation of victory. Yet for all its bile and virulence and narrative power and Milyukov's incisive style, the *Second Revolution* cannot withstand comparison with the first. It is also perhaps the case that Milyukov's interpretation of events in terms of a liberalism that consistently and unjustifiably gave more and more ground to extremists is less able than Trotsky's to understand the events of the revolution. Be that as it may, Trotsky's *History* stands alone, and survives indeed the transformation of the revolution into a very different reality from that anticipated by its author.

What of Trotsky the biographer? He remains true to himself in all his work. *On Lenin* is a book that none but Trotsky could have written. It is here presented for the first time in an accurate and complete English translation. It is slight in the context of his whole *oeuvre* but the insight it casts on the relationship between two of the most important personalities of the twentieth century gives it an importance far beyond its immediate interest. This is all the more so as Lenin remains so elusive a person. "How strange it is," wrote a Soviet author, M. Koltsov, in 1923, "we so admire, so love him, and yet know him personally so little . . . The living Lenin is even now wholly unknown and incomprehensible to us." Lenin, in Gorky's view, "knew how to be silent about the secret storms of his soul." Such reticence must make the personal testimony of Lenin's intimates all the more welcome. But such testimony will also express the man who gives it utterance. Trotsky on Lenin is also Trotsky on Trotsky.

Hence the immediate interest of this book cannot even be separated from the circumstances of its composition for these have helped to determine Trotsky's particular choice of subject-matter and its treatment.

It was always Trotsky's impulse to take to the pen and evaluate each peripateia in an agitated life. After the abortive upheaval of 1905 he wrote his *Balance and Prospects—the Motive Forces of the Revolution*. The negotiations at Brest-Litovsk, the civil war, the turning points in the early history of the Communist International—each was followed by Trotsky's exposé, assessment, analysis. Similarly, Lenin's death in January 1924 evoked the present biographical sketch. It is confessedly weak and the work of a fallible memory. Trotsky hoped that it would yet give primary evidence for the future, full biography of Lenin. Written in 1924, as it were—the very year of Trotsky's death—these notes would in the immediate future also preserve a life-like memory of Lenin and protect him from idolization.

The historical value of Trotsky's work is self-evident and ranges from the personal to the world-political. Here, as Trotsky himself says, are essentially the final six months of the *Iskra* period (1902–03) and the year and a half from mid-1917 to the autumn of 1918. It begins with the colony of Russian radicals exiled in Edwardian London, the comparatively orderly ménage of Lenin and Krupskaya in vivid contrast to the bohemian ways of Vera Zasulich and Martrov, the walks about London, the interplay of personality; then the abrupt jump to 1917 and the very centre of the political strife. Here Trotsky has many a sidelight to throw on this or that aspect of Bolshevik policy—the actual timing of the Bolshevik coup and its association with the Second Congress of Soviets; the intense controversy surrounding negotiations at Brest-Litovsk; the arguments for and against the dispersal of the Constituent Assembly; the significance of the advice on Warsaw in 1920.

The world knows many Lenins. They include Gorky's 'humanist'—the militant optimist who held that human misery was not "an inevitable condition of human existence" and could and must be overcome. They include also Balabanov's Lenin—the incorruptible egalitarian for whom there was no contradiction between the statesman and the private man. What of Trotsky's Lenin? In view of the cult to which Lenin's personality in 1924 and 1925 was already becoming subordinated, the present work is remarkably balanced. For all Trotsky's hero-worship of Lenin, this is undoubtedly the portrait of a recognizable human being, sometimes wrong, even though more frequently right. For example, Trotsky makes no attempt to conceal the erroneous decision made as a result of what he calls Lenin's "tactical élan" to advance on Warsaw in the summer of 1920. This attempt to break through the unexpected and unwelcome isolation still encompassing the Soviet Republic and sound out the possibilities of revolution in Poland, and, more particularly, Germany, foundered in catastrophe. Russia had to sign the treaty of Riga with Poland, a withdrawal that signified the end of the heroic, internationalist phase of the revolution and, within less than a year, served as prelude to a semblance of normal diplomatic relations with such major capitalist powers as Britain and Germany. Trotsky, admittedly, argues that only in hindsight did the magnitude of Lenin's error manifest itself, and he seeks to justify the advance on Warsaw by reference to "the audacity and courage of Lenin's conception." But a mistake, even if only apparent through the use of hindsight, remains objectively a mistake—however much Trotsky may try to palliate the mistake.

What stands out in Trotsky's portrait of Lenin is the latter's unmitigated and unrelenting drive to revolution and power: he had, as Trotsky writes, "only one goal before his eyes, and towards this final goal he was pressing, whether in politics or in his theoretical or philosophical studies, in discussions with others or in learning foreign languages. His was perhaps the most determined utilitarianism ever produced in the laboratory of history". How well we can comprehend Lenin's irritation with "the long palavers, formless debates and interminable chaotic conversations which inevitably led to émigré gossip and empty chatter", such as was typical of the exiled political radical. Through the contrast between Lenin and Martov, say, we see all the more clearly Lenin's "whole being geared to one great purpose. He possessed *the tenseness of striving towards* his

goal". Yes, this is the Lenin whom Trotsky presents; the
man who self-consciously yoked himself to the demands of
revolution. In a Russia starved of political personality and
greatness Lenin becomes the pendant to a Thomas Münzer,
a Luther, a Mirabeau, Danton, or Robespierre.

This is unchallengeably true. But Trotsky crosses the
frontier between the most profound and historically legitimate admiration into the romanticism of hero-worship that
far exceeds identity of aim and camaraderie in a common
struggle. From the pathos of Lenin, the lover of animals and
children, we step forward to the truly mystical concept of
Lenin as the "embodiment of the Russian proletariat."
Indeed, this is the condition of his success for "there seems
to exist between the vital forces of the country and the leader
some organic, indissoluble link deep down at the roots of his
being . . . Freedom from habit and custom, from hypocrisy
and convention, boldness of thought, audacity in action—
audacity which never becomes recklessness, are characteristic
of the Russian proletariat—and of Lenin as well."

Between pathos and a transfiguring mysticism there is a
Lenin who contrives to be both a national and an international type; Lenin "the master archer"; Lenin leading the
Bolsheviks "unfalteringly towards momentous tasks"; Lenin
who could "in every instance distinguish the essence of the
matter from the form"; Lenin who "was able to dispose of
innumerable problems during a single session" of the
Council of People's Commissars. If Lenin's speech to the
First Congress of Soviets in June 1917 "was not perhaps
quite a success from a oratorical point of view", then it was
at least "of exceptional significance"; if Lenin disregarded
all that was of secondary importance, he was still able to
comprehend a problem in "all its details, sometimes even
tertiary ones"; if he had an "enormous" respect for human
personality, he none the less subordinated it to "his respect
and solicitude for mankind as a whole." But this is not
assessment, it is pure hero-worship. Hence Trotsky's anger
at those such as Gorky or H. G. Wells who, whatever their

other faults, could at least discern the occasional flaw or tear in the Emperor's clothes. Trotsky's fulsome adulation is all the more surprising given his superlative ability to "hit off" a character in a few select phrases. His *History* abounds in such swift well-chosen strokes. But where Lenin is concerned, the sharp point of the pen is blunted. In fact, in his later writings Trotsky goes even further and attributes to Lenin an indispensable role, difficult to reconcile with traditional Marxist thought, in the successful execution of Bolshevik policy. "Had I not been present in 1917 in Petrograd," Trotsky wrote in his Diary, "the October Revolution would still have taken place—*on the condition that Lenin was present and in command.* If neither Lenin nor I had been present in Petrograd, there would have been no October Revolution: the leadership of the Bolshevik Party would have prevented it from occurring—of this I have not the slightest doubt." This may or may not be true. But that Trotsky should make such an assertion, with all its denial of the limited historical role of the individual, is indicative of his hero-worship.

Trotsky, in the present work, by no means conceals certain differences between himself and Lenin. Yet he has also chosen to describe precisely those two epochs in his life when he stood closest to Lenin, both politically and personally. This idyllic picture must, however, be complemented by some further account of what happened in the interim.

Within a year or so of the first phase described by Trotsky, he and Lenin were engaged in vituperation and invective. This arose in the initial stage from Trotsky's rejection of Lenin's model of a centralized political party formed of professional revolutionaries. Trotsky, at this time, was aligned rather with the Menshevik opposition to Lenin, saw the latter's methods as "a dull caricature of the tragic intransigence of Jacobinism." He predicted a course of degeneration in which "the party is replaced by the organization of the party; the Central Committee takes the place of the organization; and finally the dictator replaces the

Central Committee." Trotsky later repented of this analysis and, on reflection, considered Lenin's position to be "politically correct and therefore indispensable from the point of view of organization." Even so, the initial division of 1903 was the prelude to further mutual denigration. If Lenin could speak of Trotsky's "resounding but hollow phrases", of his "bombast" and scathingly assert that "it is impossible to argue with Trotsky on any point of substance since he has no opinions", then Trotsky could retaliate with a denunciation, admittedly private, of the "lying and falsification" at the root of Leninism, carrying within itself "the poisoned element of its own disintegration." Not until the spring and summer of 1917 were the two men reconciled in a partnership that brought together two of the greatest revolutionaries the world has ever seen. Not for nothing did Trotsky say that he came "fighting" to Bolshevism. He also did not do so without reflection. In May 1917, when Lenin offered Trotsky and his group of united social democrats editorial participation in the Bolshevik journal *Pravda* and a share in the organization of the imminent Bolshevik party congress, Trotsky refused, though not categorically. "The Bolsheviks have de-bolshevized themselves, and I cannot call myself a Bolshevik. It is impossible to demand of us a recognition of Bolshevism." In Lenin's view, according to Balabanov, what held Trotsky back was "ambition, ambition and more ambition." Not until another two months had passed did Trotsky and his grouping join the Bolsheviks. Even so, it required Lenin's tact and discretion to overcome what Balabanov calls "all resentments, factional animosities and his (own) personal dislike of Trotsky's behaviour" and introduce Trotsky at once into the highest echelons of the party.

Trotsky, for his part, had now linked his fate with that of Lenin and Bolshevism in general. It took him to the heights. In the conditions of 1917, Lenin and the Bolsheviks offered the only policy of upheaval that was dynamic enough to appeal to Trotsky's own zest for action. Only they could make an ambitious response to the exigencies of the moment.

For the next four years or so no two men in the Central
Committee of the Bolshevik Party stood closer than Lenin
and Trotsky. These two names in themselves embodied to
an alarmed and astonished world the militant threat of the
revolution. In an endeavour to provide harmoniously for his
succession, Lenin offered Trotsky the deputy chairmanship
of the Council of Ministers, and in March 1923 it was to
Trotsky to whom the dying Lenin turned in despair to
present his views on the crucial Georgian question.

It is thus clear how incomplete and one-sided is Trotsky's
presentation of his relationship to Lenin. This is not fortuitous. On the one hand, it must be remembered that Trotsky
was a newcomer to Bolshevism. He had, as it were, to work
his passage. "He was the neophyte," writes Balabanov, "who
wanted to outdo in zeal and ardour the Bolsheviks themselves, the neophyte who wanted to be forgiven the many
crimes against Bolshevism he had committed in the past—
by becoming a greater royalist than the king, by becoming
more intransigent, more revolutionary, more Bolshevik than
any of them. He avoided everything that held even the
remotest possibility of his being taken for a Menshevik."

Second, it must also be remembered that even before
Lenin's death, Trotsky's star was already on the wane. It is
true, of course, that Lenin's own appreciation was in no way
undimmed, as the offer of deputy chairmanship of the
Council of Ministers abundantly testifies. In his *Testament*,
indeed, Lenin terms Trotsky one of "the most eminent
leaders in the present Central Committee." He was "the
most able" of the party leaders, although possessed by "too
great a self-confidence", by temperament "over-attracted to
the purely administrative side of affairs" and his individual-
ism led him to oppose himself to the will of the Central
Committee.

However despite, or perhaps because of, these very qualities Trotsky's decline coincided with Lenin's enforced withdrawal from the scene of action. It was not only a question
of the fear generated by Trotsky's supposed "Napoleonic"

proclivities but also of the "old guard" closing its ranks against a talented newcomer. With the deterioration in Lenin's health in 1922 and even more so in 1923, he came to depend more and more on the triumvirate formed of Stalin, Zinoviev, and Kamenev. Trotsky understood this well enough and writes in his autobiography:

> There is no doubt that in routine work it was more convenient for Lenin to depend on Stalin, Zinoviev or Kamenev rather than on me. Lenin was always trying to save his time as well as everyone else's. He tried to reduce to a minimum the energy spent in overcoming friction. I had my own views, my own ways of working, and my own methods of carrying out a decision once it had been adopted. Lenin knew this well enough, and respected it. That was why he understood only too well that I was not suited for executing commissions. When he needed men to carry out his instructions, he turned to someone else. In certain periods, especially when Lenin and I had had a disagreement, this probably made his assistants believe that they were particularly close to him.

There is also a sense in which it can be said that Lenin's gradual enfeeblement, coinciding as it did with the emergence of some sort of truce between the Soviet republic and the capitalist world, made Trotsky's particular gifts less essential—or seem so, at least. Of course, it was purely fortuitous that the relative internal and external consolidation of Soviet rule should coincide with Lenin's enforced retirement from action through physical causes. Yet these factors, combined with the early stages of that 'bureaucratic deformation' to which Trotsky himself attributed so much importance, worked together to weaken Trotsky's position. It is in the perspective of this situation that Trotsky, in this biography, should naturally—perhaps inevitably—take to recounting the heyday of his association with Lenin.

Trotsky's relative isolation and his relationship to Lenin can also be seen and understood in the perspective of his

Jewish origin. The latter was certainly not the condition of the former, but they were equally certainly connected. Trotsky, like the other radical Jews of his generation inside and outside Russia, *e.g.*, Luxemburg, Victor Adler, Martov, Otto Bauer, not only, of course, scorned Judaism as a religion, but also saw no prospect of a separate Jewish existence, for which the only solution lay in social revolution, assimilation and an allegiance to internationalism. "Disdain and even a moral nausea"—this is the way in which Trotsky describes his reaction to nationalism. "My marxist education deepened this feeling, and changed my attitude to that of an active internationalism. My life in so many countries, my acquaintance with so many different languages, political systems and cultures, only helped me to absorb that internationalism into my very flesh and blood."

So far as Russia itself was concerned, although those Marxists of Jewish origin were frequently at political odds with each other, they shared the important negative characteristic of hailing from *outside* the densely populated areas of the Jewish Pale of Settlement in the Western provinces of the Empire,[1] Trotsky himself was born in a village in the Ukraine and attended school in Odessa; Martov was born in Constantinople and taken to Odessa at the age of four; Kamenev was born in Moscow and educated at Vilna and Tiflis; Zinoviev was born in Elizavetgrad (former province of Kherson).

But it was not sufficient for these men and their like to be subjectively internationalists; it was also necessary to be accepted as such. In this Trotsky was less successful and the fact of his Jewish origin took an inescapable part in his career. It was precisely for this reason, for example, that Trotsky was deputed by Lenin to lead the assault on the *Bund*—the Jewish Marxist party—at the Second (London) Congress of the Russian Social Democratic Party in 1903.

---

[1] We lack a detailed study of Jewish participation in Russian political life on the scale *e.g.* of J. Toury's *Die politischen Orientierungen der Juden in Deutschland* (Tübingen, 1966).

It was, in part, due to precisely the same factor that Trotsky found himself, in 1917, Commissar for foreign and not domestic affairs; and it was, of course, only because of his origin that the weapon of anti-semitism could be used against him in the struggle for power that followed Lenin's death.

Internationalism, however sincerely adhered to, did not, in short, give the answer to Trotsky's ambivalent position. On the contrary, it may even have contributed to his isolation, as it certainly did to his downfall.

In general terms it is clear enough that during the decade or so before 1917 Lenin's ascendancy amongst the Bolsheviks expressed itself, in terms of personality, in the gradual movement of the more theoretical and speculative intellects amongst the Russian Marxists into the ranks of Menshevism or some intermediate grouping (*e.g.* Plekhanov, Martov) or even further to the right (Struve). The process of moulding the Bolsheviks into a force able to make a bid for power necessarily required a responsive instrument, *i.e.*, one responsive to Lenin's views. Of course, this did not prevent or inhibit the most intense controversy inside the party. But it was for the most part within the framework set by the current political situation—tactics in 1917, to accept or reject Brest-Litovsk, the role of the trade unions, etc. In effect, however, the party had lost a considerable degree of freedom in discussion. New tasks obviously required a new approach. There is nothing surprising in this. The more earnestly that actual political tasks confronted the Bolsheviks, the more narrowly did controversy have to content itself with seeking means to perform those tasks.

What is significant is that this process was accompanied, inevitably, by a change in personnel of a type necessarily uncongenial to a cosmopolitan intellectual of Jewish origins, as exemplified in Trotsky. Of course, it would be absurd to identify cosmopolitanism and intellectuality solely with those Bolsheviks of Jewish origin. But it would be equally absurd to claim that the activity of these latter did not give the party a special flavour compounded of these attributes.

Their elimination can be observed, for example, through a scrutiny of those 17 members of the Central Committee elected after 1920 for the first time.[2] They included only one Jew (Karl Radek) though over one-third were of non-Russian extraction. Almost three-quarters were of peasant stock and over 40% had had only an elementary education. As against this, the members of earlier Central Committees were distinguished by a greater proportion of men of middle-class origin, with a higher educational attainment and a higher proportion of Jews amongst the large number of those of non-Russian extraction. This was a representative picture of the personnel elected to the seven central committees formed between May 1917 and March–April 1922.

The same over-all analysis is also derived from an examination of a larger sample of leading Bolsheviks. It has been shown that two separate generations of Bolsheviks can be said to have reached political maturity in the years between 1917 and 1922. There was that generation born between 1868 and 1874 (40) and that born between 1883 and 1891 (103). Again, pronounced differences separate the two groups in terms of ethnic origin, social background, and educational attainment. Thus, in the first group, dominance is claimed by those who were of non-Russian extraction, came from a middle-class background and enjoyed a higher or secondary education. There was in fact none with an elementary education.

The younger group, on the other hand, contained a higher proportional representation of Russians, of lower-class background with an elementary education. This change did not affect the central leadership of the party (*i.e.* those eight party members who sat in at least six of the seven Central Committees elected between 1917 and 1922). But it did appear in the Central Committee as a whole, and it is embodied in Stalin "the prototype and, at the same time,

---

[2] For the following data I am indebted to W. E. Mosse, *Makers of the Soviet Union*, Slavonic and East European Review, Vol. 46, 1968.

the forerunner of the 'new men' ".[3] Both Stalin and Trotsky were born in 1879. But whereas, by 1924 say, the one belonged to the future, the other belonged to the past.

This is the past that Trotsky seeks to re-capture and in so doing, to establish his credentials as an Old Bolshevik, although he only joined the party in 1917 and had spent the previous decade in opposition to it. He idealizes Lenin, he harks back to their days in common harness, he portrays his dependence on Lenin—"my master", he calls him in his autobiography. To no avail. The Central Committee was progressively shedding its international-revolutionary character.

Events, internationally, reinforced this tendency. It certainly cannot be said that the triumvirate of Stalin, Kamenev and Zinoviev conducted affairs more capably than Trotsky would have done. But the fact is that Stalin at least showed greater sensitivity to extra-Russian affairs than Trotsky. His cautious, perhaps even pessimistic, attitude to the possibility of a German revolution in 1923 clearly showed this. Trotsky, on the other hand, deeply involved himself in the fortunes of German Communism and suffered correspondingly when it proved a fiasco. This was not all—the German failure was only symptomatic of some return to stability in post-war Europe. This in its turn found expression in the slow development of some degree of normality in the diplomatic and economic relations encompassing Soviet Russia and the capitalist world. 'The Year of Recognitions'—1924—to say nothing of the ever closer relationship with Germany was the natural setting and context for the enunciation of Stalin's doctrine of "socialism in one country". At a time of unwelcome revolutionary ebb, this gave Bolshevik Russia a *raison d'être* which it would otherwise in part have lacked. It also contrasted favourably with Trotsky's continued commitment to an ever-receding international revolution. Later, of course, Trotsky's insight into the consequences of a Nazi victory proved incomparably more perceptive than Stalin's

---

[8] Mosse, *op. cit.*, p. 152.

blindness. But ten years earlier this had not been the case.

What then remains? For this it is necessary to look beyond Trotsky's fate as an individual, even that of the Soviet Union, and still more that of the Fourth International. What remains is the reality of an incorruptible man, true to himself in all his varied activities—as revolutionary, literary critic, orator, man of war, political thinker. Equally enduring is Trotsky's stature as historian. *The History of the Russian Revolution* brings together all those qualities that distinguish the historian as a man. Here is indeed an achievement that counterpoises his relative failure as a man of action. The present work stands forth clearly as the product of the same Pen.

Publishing History

TROTSKY'S *On Lenin* has been something of a 'lost' book so far as English-reading audiences are concerned. It is frequently omitted from bibliographies of source material on the Russian Revolution and in lists of Trotsky's work. A partial explanation of this appears from an examination of the book's publishing history.

As Trotsky says in his foreword, his aim was to gather materials for a future biographer of Lenin and he indicates that he intended to write one himself. When the book first appeared the publishers must have regarded it as something that would soon be replaced by a work of a more permanent nature. In Russia, the original edition was published by the State Publishing House in 1924 in an edition of 30,000 copies. It disappeared from circulation fairly soon after as

the author fell further from favour. An edition appeared in
Paris the following year under the imprint of Libraire du
Travail and at about the same time the New York house of
Minton, Balch acquired English-language rights. An 'authorized translation' came out accompanied by an anonymous
publisher's note claiming that the book was one of the
principal causes of Trotsky's exile—which modern scholar-
ship would scarcely sustain. The translation is a rather curious
one and contains a number of startling errors—at one stage
Lenin is credited with having made the sign of the cross in a
moment of tension and at another Trotsky's rather rhetorical
"It seems that here is a self-educated man . . ." (p. 139) is
rendered as "Does it not seem as though an extraordinary
auto-dictator were speaking . . ." The question arises—who
authorized the translation? The records for this period in
New York seem to have vanished and the only comment one
can make is that Trotsky's usual translator, Max Eastman,
obviously had no hand in the matter.

The American translation appeared in London published
by Harrap in 1925.

And there the matter rested. Harrap, like the other
involved publishers, waited to see if Trotsky would prepare
a complete biography of Lenin. It was not until 1940 and
Trotsky's assassination that it became clear that the biography
would never be written. In fact, Trotsky's intention was for
a three-part work. The first and only of these, dealing with
Lenin's youth, was written in the middle thirties and
appeared in France under the title *Jeunesse* in 1936. An
English translation by Max Eastman exists but had not
appeared by the end of 1970. But by 1940, interest in Trotsky was at an all-time low. During World War II there were
fears of disturbing the alliance with Russia and afterwards,
during the Cold War, there was interest only in works which
showed Russia in a bad light. It was on this basis that
Trotsky's biography of Stalin, completed in 1940 and ready
for publication in 1941, appeared in 1946.

So Trotsky's *On Lenin*, of importance now by default,

became forgotten. When in the middle of 1969 it reappeared in Harrap's editorial library (it was in fact lucky to survive bombing during World War II), a fairly formidable publishing task arose. Had Harrap's any right to reissue the work?

Harrap's original right derived from their 1924 contract with Minton, Balch, but that firm had long since disappeared. Who were their successors, and what rights did they in fact control? Even today, works of Russian origin cause western publishers problems, as the USSR is not a party to any of the internationally recognized copyright conventions. Normally a British or American publisher takes the precaution of issuing a Russian-language edition of any book he wishes to publish shortly before the English translation appears and this is generally regarded as giving him a good title to the work. However, none of this can apply to a book which already appeared in 1925. The situation is further complicated by the facts of Trotsky's own history—did he in fact have any protection at all, and if so, from which legal system? Further still, was there a disparity between the American and British position and did the 1925 contract have validity today only so far as the mysterious 'authorized translation' was concerned leaving aside the rights in the underlying work?

Eventually the Trotsky estate was contacted and it was agreed that royalties should be paid to its Paris representatives.

The copyright and contractual situation took some six months to sort out but as a result this key source book can now take its rightful place in the literature.

Foreword

THIS book is in two respects incomplete. First of all one should look here neither for a biography of Lenin, nor for a study of his character, nor for a full survey of his views and methods of action. This volume provides only some materials, the outlines and sketches for future work—perhaps even for future work by the author of these lines. This somewhat 'sketchy' approach is both inevitable and necessary. In addition to the popular biographies and more general character studies, there is already now the need to set down on paper with more care and attention certain episodes, certain moments in Lenin's life and particular features of his personality as we were able to observe them with our own eyes. The greater part of this book consists of memories of two periods between which fifteen years elapsed: the last six months of the old *Iskra* period and the decisive year of the October upheaval: that is, to be more precise, the period from the middle of 1917 till autumn 1918.

This book is not complete in another, and narrower, sense of the word: I hope that circumstances will allow me to continue this work, to improve on it, to correct it, to make it more accurate, to expand it, and add new episodes and new chapters. Temporary withdrawal from day-to-day work, due to illness, helped me to recall much of what is related here. Later, while reading my first notes, the skein of memories began to unwind and further reminiscences unravelled new episodes which were interesting if only because they were connected with Lenin and with his life. However, this method of work has its disadvantage: the product is never finished. This is why at a certain point I decided to cut short the manuscript and to publish it in incomplete form. But, as I said before, I reserve to myself the right to continue work on this book, and it goes without saying that I should be most grateful to any and all of those who witnessed the events described if they came forward with corrections or if they brought to it some new memories. It should be said, however, that I have left out deliberately a whole range of episodes because they are still too closely connected with present-day affairs.

To the two main parts of the book consisting of reminiscences, I have added those articles, essays, and speeches (or fragments of speeches), in which my purpose was to give a characterization of Lenin.

Working over these memories I used hardly any documents referring to the period with which I have dealt. It seemed to me that as it was not my aim to present a full-scale historical narrative of any particular phase of Lenin's life, but only to give some first-hand source material such as precisely I can provide, it would be better to rely on my own memory.

I had practically finished writing this book, when I read volume XIV of Lenin's *Works* and the book on the Brest-Litovsk peace by Comrade Ovsyannikov; the additions which resulted from this reading were very few indeed.

L. Trotsky

P.S. On re-reading the manuscript I noticed that in my reminiscences I refer to the city of Leningrad either as Petrograd or Petersburg. Some comrades give to the old Petrograd retrospectively the name Leningrad. This does not seem correct to me. Can one say, for example, that Lenin was arrested in Leningrad? It is obvious that this would sound very strange. Even less possible would be to say: Peter I founded Leningrad. One can imagine that as years and decades go by the new name of a city, like all other proper names, will lose its vivid historical meaning. But for the

time being we are still too much aware that Petrograd became Leningrad after January 21st 1924—and it could not
have been so re-named earlier. And this is why I preserve
the name of the city current at the time of the events I recall.

L.T.

April 21st, 1924

1
Lenin and the old Iskra

"The split of 1903 was, so
to speak, an anticipation . . ."
(Lenin in 1910)

THERE is no doubt that to the future great biographer
of Lenin the old *Iskra* period (1900–03) will be of
unique psychological interest, and also of considerable
difficulty: it was precisely during this short time that Lenin
became the Lenin he was to remain. This does not mean that
he did not develop further. On the contrary. He grew in
stature—and at what a rate—until October and after; but
this was really organic growth. The leap from illegality to
the seizure of power on October 25th 1917 was enormous;
but this was, so to speak, outward, the shooting upward of
a man who had already weighed and measured all it was
possible to weigh and measure, while in the growth which
occurred before the split at the Second Congress of the Party
there was the imperceptible, and all the more fundamental
inward development.

The aim of these reminiscences is to give the future biographer some material which would throw light on this
memorable and significant period in the spiritual development of Vladimir Ilyich. From that time to the present
moment of writing over two decades have passed, two
decades crowding human memory quite exceptionally. This
may give rise to certain doubts: how far is what is related
here a correct presentation of past events? I must admit that
I myself was prey to these doubts all through the process of
writing. Already there are too many incoherent 'memoirs'

and inexact eye-witness accounts. When I drafted this essay I had no documents and no reference material to hand whatsoever. I think that, on balance, this was all to the good. I had to rely on my memory alone, and I hope that this gave my work more spontaneity and also made it free from that unconscious retrospective touching-up which it is so difficult to avoid, even with the utmost self-discipline and self-criticism. Moreover, my writings will facilitate the sifting of evidence in future research which will be done with all the available files and documents dealing with the past.

In some passages I reconstruct conversations and debates and present them in the form of a dialogue. Of course, it is impossible to pretend that discussions which took place twenty odd years ago are reproduced word for word. But in substance, I trust, I have related them faithfully and in the case of a particularly lively exchange of words, literally.

As we are concerned here with material for a future biographer of Lenin, and so with a matter of paramount importance, I would like to be permitted to make a few remarks about certain qualities of my memory. I remember very badly the topography of cities and even of houses. In London, for example, more than once I lost my way in the relatively short distance which separated my lodgings from those of Lenin. For a long time I had a poor memory for faces, but in this respect I have made considerable progress. On the other hand, I have always had—and still have—an excellent memory for ideas, their flow and associations, and for discussions about ideas.

That this assessment of my memory is not subjective I have been able to verify on many occasions: other people present with me at some debate, have related it with much less precision than I did, and they have accepted my corrections. One should, however, add that young provincial that I was on arriving in London, I was eager to learn everything and to see everything as rapidly as possible. No wonder that the talks with Lenin and other members of the editorial board of *Iskra* engraved themselves on my memory. Such, then, are the circumstances which a future biographer will have to take into account in determining the degree of trustworthiness of recollections published below.

I arrived in London in the autumn of 1902, I think in October, very early in the morning. With signs and gestures I managed to hire a cab which took me to the address written on a piece of paper. My destination was the lodging of Vladimir Ilyich. I was taught in advance (it must have been still in Zürich) to knock on the door a certain prescribed number of times. As far as I remember Nadezhda Konstantinovna opened the door; I must have dragged her out of bed by my knocking. It was very early in the morning; a man more experienced and more accustomed, so to speak, to a civilized way of life, would have stayed quietly at the station an hour or two instead of knocking on strangers' doors at the crack of dawn. But I was still full of the excitement of my escape from Verkholensk. I had descended on Axelrod's household in Zürich in more or less the same manner— not at dawn, but in the middle of the night.

Vladimir Ilyich was still in bed and his face expressed kindness tinged with justifiable amazement. In such circumstances our first meeting and our first talk took place. Vladimir Ilyich and Nadezhda Konstantinovna knew about me already through a letter from Clair (M. G. Kzhizhanovsky) who introduced me officially into the *Iskra* organization in Samara under the pseudonym Pen. And that is how I was greeted: "Hey, Pen has arrived!". . . . I was given tea, in the kitchen-dining room, I think. In the meantime Lenin got dressed. I told them about my escape and complained about the bad state of the *Iskra* 'frontier',[1] which was managed by a college boy, an SR[2] who was unsympathetic to the *Iskra* group as a result of bitter polemics which had just flared up. Besides, smugglers had fleeced me shamelessly, raising all their tariffs and rates. I handed over to Nadezhda

---

[1] Point of illegal crossing of the frontier.
[2] Member of the Social Revolutionary Party.

Konstantinovna a modest batch of addresses and a list of meeting points, or, to be more exact, I informed her of the necessity of doing away with some addresses which had become valueless. On behalf of the Samara group (Clair and others) I had visited Kharkov, Poltava, Kiev, and practically everywhere, but certainly in Kharkov and Poltava, I found that the organizational links were extremely defective.

The same morning, or perhaps next day, I went for a long walk with Vladimir Ilyich. He showed me Westminster Abbey (from outside) and some other architectural landmarks. I do not remember how he actually said it, but the inflection in his voice meant, "That's *their* famous Westminster". 'Their' meant not, of course, the one belonging to the English, but to the enemy. This inflection in Lenin's voice, apparently accidental, was organically his own; it was this tone which always made its appearance when Lenin spoke about some cultural treasures or new achievements, about the arrangements of the British Museum, about the wealth of information contained in *The Times*, and also, many years later, about German artillery or the French air force: *they* know, *they* have got, *they* made it, *they* achieved —yes, but what foes *they* are! In his eyes the shadow of the exploiting classes lay over the whole human culture and this shadow was always as visible to him as daylight.

As far as I can remember, I showed a very slight interest in the architecture of London at the time. Suddenly transported from Verkholensk, straight out of Russia—I found myself abroad for the first time—I was taking in Vienna, Paris, and London in a rather summary manner and could hardly notice such 'details' as Westminster Abbey. Besides, Vladimir Ilyich had something else in mind when he took me for the long walk. He wanted to get to know me and to examine me. And indeed 'the whole *curriculum*' became the subject of the examination. Answering his questions, I described the composition of the colony of deportees on the Lena and the inner groupings which were forming themselves. The main line of division between various tendencies was marked by the attitude towards active political struggle, towards the principle of centralism in the organization, and towards terrorism.

"Well, and were there no theoretical differences of opinion in connection with Bernstein's views?" asked Vladimir Ilyich. I told him how we read Bernstein's book and Kautsky's reply to it in the Moscow prison and later on in exile. In our group none of the Marxists sided with Bernstein. It was taken for granted that Kautsky's view was the correct one. But we did not see any connection between the theoretical struggle then proceeding on an international scale and our organizational-political quarrels; we did not even give a thought to the idea that there might be a connection between the two, at least not until the first copies of *Iskra* and Lenin's book *What is to be Done?* appeared in the Lena colonies. I told him that we had read the first philosophical works of Bogdanov[3] with great interest. I remember very clearly Vladimir Ilyich's remark: he also thought that the little book on nature written from the materialistic point of view was very valuable, but, well, Plekhanov did not approve of it saying that this was not materialism. Vladimir Ilyich had no definite opinion yet on the subject, he only related Plekhanov's views with great respect for his authority on philosophical matters, but also with some uneasiness. I, too, was amazed at Plekhanov's assessment of the book.

Then Vladimir Ilyich asked some question on economics. I told him how in the Moscow transfer prison we studied collectively his volume on *The Development of Capitalism in Russia*, and how in exile we worked over *Das Kapital* stopping, however, at the second volume. I remarked on the tremendous amount of statistical data processed in *The Development of Capitalism*. In the Moscow prison we commented many a time on this massive work.

"Yes, but this was not done all at once," answered Lenin.

---

[3] Bogdanov, (Malinovsky), Alexander Alexandrovich (1873–1928), philosopher and economist, from 1896 a Social Democrat, in 1903 joined the Bolsheviks. (Translator's note.)

Obviously it gave him pleasure to learn that young comrades paid great attention to his most important book on economics.

Then we talked about Makhaisky[4] and about the impression his theory had made on the exiles, and about those who succumbed to it. I told him that the first hectographed pamphlet by Makhaisky to reach us on the Lena came from 'high up' and made quite an impact on the majority of people because of its violent critique of social-democratic opportunism; in this sense it accorded well with our way of thinking provoked by the Kautsky-Bernstein polemic. The second pamphlet in which Makhaisky 'tears down the mask' of Marx's formulation of production laws, seeing in it a theoretical justification for the exploitation of the proletariat by the intelligentsia, aroused our indignation and caused confusion. Finally, we received the third pamphlet, containing a positive programme in which the remnants of 'economism' were mixed up with the germs of syndicalism. This seemed to us completely incoherent.

We talked about my future work with Lenin but only in the most general terms. First of all, I wanted to acquaint myself with what had been published recently, and then I intended to return illegally to Russia. It was decided that I should, for the time being, 'look around' a little.

I had to find some lodgings, and Nadezhda Konstantinovna took me to another district of London, to a house where Vera Zasulich and Martov lived, and also Blumenfeld who was in charge of the *Iskra* printing shop. There was a room vacant there which I took. The house was typically English: the living space was organized not horizontally but vertically, with the owner living on the lowest floor, and the lodgers living one over the other. There was one common room which Plekhanov, on his very first visit, nicknamed 'the den'. Mostly because of Vera Zasulich, but not without

---

[4] V. K. Makhaisky (A. Volski), a Polish socialist-anarchist, hostile to Marxism and ultra-critical towards the intelligentsia presenting it as a 'parasite class'.

the active cooperation of Martov, this room was always in a state of terrible disorder. Here we drank coffee, met for palavers, smoked, and so on.

This was how the short period of my London existence began. I threw myself avidly into the copies of *Iskra* and the pamphlets of *Zaria*. At this time too, I began to work on *Iskra*. I think that my first contribution to *Iskra* consisted of a note on the occasion of the twentieth anniversary of the Schlüsselburg fortress. The note ended with a quotation from Homer, or rather from Homer's Russian translator Gnedich, about the "invincible hands" with which the revolution would take Tsarism in its grip (on the way from Siberia I had read the *Iliad* very thoroughly). Lenin liked the note. But he had some legitimate doubts about those "invincible hands" and expressed them to me with a benevolent smile. "But this is a quotation from Homer", I said to justify myself, yet I readily agreed that the classical quotation was not indispensable. My note can be found in the *Iskra*, but without the "invincible hands".

It was then also that I gave my first lectures in Whitechapel, where I had to join battle with the 'old' Tchaikovsky (he was by then an old man) and with the anarchist Tcherkezov, who was not a young man either. I was sincerely astonished that such famous grey-bearded émigrés were capable of talking such complete nonsense. . . The Marxist émigré Alexeev, who was an 'old Londoner' and was in close contact with the *Iskra* people, became my link with Whitechapel. It was he who introduced me into the 'English way of life' and, generally speaking, became for me the 'fount of all knowledge' in this field.

I remember a particular conversation I had with him on our way to Whitechapel and back; I repeated to Vladimir Ilyich the two views which Alexeev expressed, one on the manner in which the change in the Russian political regime would occur, and the other on the last book by Kautsky. "In Russia," said Alexeev, "the change will not come about gradually, but rather violently, precisely as a result of the *rigidity*[5] of autocracy." The word *rigidity* (rudeness, hard-ness, inflexibility) engraved itself on my memory. "Well," said Lenin, "he may be right, after all."

The second was Alexeev's opinion about Kautsky's work *On the Morrow of the Social Revolution.* I knew that Lenin was very interested in the book and that, as he said himself, he had read it twice over and was reading it for the third time; it seemed to me that he even revised the Russian translation. As for myself, I had just finished perusing it diligently on the recommendation of Vladimir Ilyich. Alexeev, incidentally, maintained that Kautsky's work was 'opportunistic'.

"Id-iot", Lenin said unexpectedly, pouting his lips angrily—always a sign of his displeasure.

Alexeev's attitude towards Lenin was very respectful: "I think he is more important for the revolution than Plek-hanov." I did not, of course, mention this to Lenin, but I repeated Alexeev's words to Martov who did not react, however.

The editorial board of *Iskra* and *Zaria* consisted, as we know, of six people: three 'old' members, that is Plekhanov, Zasulich, and Axelrod, and three young ones, Lenin, Mar-tov, and Potresov. Plekhanov and Axelrod lived in Switzer-land and Vera Zasulich in London with the young members. Potresov was at that time somewhere on the continent. This dispersal caused technical difficulties, which did not worry Lenin however; on the contrary, he seemed to be quite pleased.

Before my departure for the continent Lenin initiated me delicately into the internal affairs of the editorial board; he also told me that Plekhanov insisted that all the editors should move to Switzerland, but that he, Lenin, was against the transfer because this would only make work more diffi-cult. This remark made me aware for the first time that the editorial board remained in London not only because of

---

[5] In English in the original.

police regulations but also for personal and organizational reasons.

In day-to-day political work Lenin sought the maximum independence from the 'old' members and principally from Plekhanov, with whom he was already in serious conflict especially over the elaboration of the party programme. The mediators in such cases were Vera Zasulich and Martov. In this duel Zasulich played the role of Plekhanov's second, and Martov that of Lenin's. Both mediators were of a conciliatory disposition and very friendly towards each other. Only gradually did I learn about the sharp clashes which occurred between Plekhanov and Lenin when they tried to work out the theoretical parts of the Party programme. I remember that Vladimir Ilyich asked my opinion on this programme, which had just been published (in *Iskra*, No. 25, if I am not mistaken). I had, however, read the programme only in its broad outlines, so that I was unable to answer the more specific questions which were of interest to Lenin. The disagreements concerned the necessity—in Lenin's view—of defining more decisively and categorically the character of capitalism and its tendencies; the concentration of production; the decline of the intermediate strata; class differentiation, and so on. . . . Plekhanov treated these subjects with more reserve and less sharply. The programme, as we know, is sprinkled with expressions such as 'more or less' which came from Plekhanov's pen.

As far as I remember, Martov and Zasulich told me that the first draft which Lenin wrote as a counter to Plekhanov's, met with the latter's harsh judgment and haughty sneers, so characteristic of him in such circumstances. Of course, this was not the way either to discourage Lenin or to intimidate him. Their struggle took quite a dramatic turn. Vera Ivanovna (Zasulich) herself repeated what she used to say to Lenin: "George (Plekhanov) is like a greyhound: he will shake you and shake you and will let you go; you are like a bulldog; you have a deadly grip." I remember this and also Vera's final remark: "He (Lenin) was very pleased. 'So I

have a deadly grip, have I?' he asked delightedly." Telling
the story Vera, with amusement, imitated Lenin's intonation.

During my stay in London Plekhanov came over for a
short trip. I saw him then for the first time. He came to our
common lodgings and to our 'den', but I was not at home.

"George has arrived", announced Vera Ivanovna. "He
wants to see you; go to his room."

"Which George?" I asked intrigued, thinking that there
must be some famous personality still unknown to me.

"Well, Plekhanov. . . . We call him George."

I went to see him in the evening. In a small room I found
him in the company of a well-known German social democratic writer, Beer, and an Englishman, Askew. All the
chairs were occupied, and Plekhanov, not without hesitation, proposed that I should sit on the bed. I took this as a
matter of course, without realizing that for Plekhanov,
every inch a European, such unconventionalities of behaviour
were permissible only in extreme circumstances. The talk
was in German in which Plekhanov was not fluent enough;
he answered in monosyllables only. Beer talked first about
the clever way in which the English bourgeoisie wins over
the most outstanding workers; then the discussion touched
on the English forerunners of French materialism. Beer and
Askew left soon afterwards. George Valentinovich expected,
not unreasonably, that I would leave with them. It was
already late and we were anxious not to disturb the neigh-
bours. But for me, on the contrary, the real conversation
was about to begin.

"What Beer said was quite interesting," I started.

"Yes, what he said about English politics was interesting,
but what he said about philosophy was trash," answered
Plekhanov.

As I was not making a move to take myself off, George
Valentinovich proposed that we should go out for a glass of
beer. He asked me a few unimportant questions, was
amiable, but in his amiability there was a trace of concealed
impatience. I felt that his attention was on other things. It

was possible that he was simply tired after the journey. But I parted from him with a feeling of dissatisfaction and irritation.

During the London period, as well as later in Geneva, I used to meet Zasulich and Martov much more often than Lenin. In London, living in the same house, and in Geneva, eating in the same small restaurants, Zasulich, Martov, and I used to see each other several times a day, while with Lenin, who led more of a family life, every meeting, apart from official gatherings, became something of a minor event.

Vera Zasulich was an exceptional person; she was also charming in a peculiar manner. She wrote very slowly, truly suffering all the torments of creation. "Vera does not write", Vladimir Ilyich once said. "She composes a mosaic." She did, indeed, put down on paper one sentence at a time, pacing up and down her room, shuffling in her slippers, chain-smoking cigarettes which she rolled herself, throwing butts in all corners of the room, on the window sills, on the table, scattering ash over her blouse, her arms, her manuscript, her tea, and incidentally also over her interlocutor. She was, and she remained to the end, the old type of radical intellectual with Marxism grafted on to her by fate. Her articles proved that she had assimilated remarkably well the theoretical elements of Marxism; but at the same time the moral-political foundations of a Russian radical of the 1870s persisted in her untouched. In more intimate talks she allowed herself to question some assumptions or conclusions of Marxism. The word 'revolutionary' had for her a particular meaning devoid of any connotation of class consciousness. I remember the talk we had about her 'Revolutionaries among the Bourgeoisie'. I used the expression 'bourgeois-democratic revolutionaries'. "Well, no", interjected Vera with annoyance, or rather with sorrow, "no, neither bourgeois nor proletarian but simply revolutionaries. One can, of course, say '*petty-bourgeois* revolutionaries,'" she added, "if one includes into petty-bourgeoisie all that one cannot place anywhere else. . . ."

At that time the ideological centre of Social Democracy was Germany, and we were watching tensely the struggle between the orthodox Social Democrats and the revisionists. But Vera Ivanovna, who thought little of all this, would say suddenly:

"Well, well. They will finish with revisionism, they will re-establish Marx, they will get a majority and in spite of it all they will live with their Kaiser."

"Which 'they', Vera Ivanovna?"

"Well, the German Social Democrat, of course."

On this point, incidentally, her judgment proved more correct than it seemed at the time, although things happened in a different way and for different reasons from those she expected.

She viewed sceptically the plan to deal with the 'cut off lands'[6]—not that she rejected it, but she treated it with a great deal of good humour.

I remember the following episode. Shortly before the Congress, Konstantin Konstantinovich Bauer came to Geneva. He was one of the old Marxists, a rather unbalanced man, who at one time had been a friend of Struve, but who now hesitated between *Iskra* and the *Osvobozhdzhenie*.[7] In Geneva he became more attracted to *Iskra*, but refused to accept the plan dealing with 'cut off lands'. He went to see Lenin, whom he probably knew already. He returned unconverted, however, maybe because Lenin, knowing his Hamlet-like doubts, did not bother to convert him. I knew Bauer from the period of exile and I now had a very long discussion with him about this unfortunate distribution of land. With the sweat of my brow I set forth all the arguments which I had managed to assemble during the six months of endless debate with the Social Revolutionaries and

---

[6] 'Cut off lands' (Russian term—*otrezki*), lands seized by the landlords from the peasants' allotments at the time of the emancipation of the serfs in 1861. (Translator's note.)

[7] *Emancipation*—a group to which Miliukov, Struve, and Prokopovich belonged. (Translator's note.)

all the other opponents of the agrarian programme of *Iskra*. And then, that very evening, Martov (I think it was Martov) announced at the meeting of the editorial board, in my presence, that Bauer had come to him and declared himself finally to be an *Iskra* man. "Well, well, Trotsky scattered to the winds all his doubts...."

"And about 'cut off lands' as well?" Vera Zasulich inquired anxiously.

"Especially about that."

"Poor chap!" she exclaimed with such a comic intonation that we all burst out laughing.

"With Vera Ivanovna much is built on moral foundations, on sentiments", Lenin said one day. Both she and Martov, Lenin went on, were sometimes tempted to defend terrorist methods, for example when Val, the Governor of Vilna, ordered workers who took part in a demonstration to be flogged. Traces of this particular 'deviation', as we would now have called it, can be found in one of the copies of *Iskra*. This is how, I think, it had happened: Martov and Zasulich were editing a copy of the paper while Lenin was on the continent. Telegraphic agencies brought a report about the flogging in Vilna. This awakened in Vera Ivanovna memories of the old heroic radical who shot Trepov because he ordered the birching of political prisoners. Martov supported her.... Lenin, when he received the fresh copy of *Iskra*, was indignant:

"This is the first step on the road to the capitulation before the Social Revolutionaries and their doctrine!"

At the same time Plekhanov sent his protest. This incident had taken place before my arrival in London so that in what I am relating here there might be some factual inaccuracies. But I remember very well the essentials of the affair.

"Of course, it is not a matter of adopting terrorism as a method," Vera Zasulich tried to explain, "but it seems to me that perhaps terrorism may teach them not to flog people...."

Vera could not really conduct a serious debate—even less

could she speak in public. She never answered her opponent's argument directly; she muttered something to herself and then, all aflame, she whirled out of herself a profusion of sentences, so fast that she was nearly choking; and she addressed herself not to the person who had questioned her, but to someone who, she hoped, would be able to understand her.

If discussion was more formal, with a chairman, Vera Zasulich never asked for the inclusion of her name on the list of speakers; in order to say something she had to be in a state of fever. But then she would hold forth without paying any attention to the formal procedure, which she treated with utter contempt: she always interrupted the speaker and the chairman and would go on talking until she had said what was on her mind. In order to understand her one had to follow her trend of thought closely; her ideas—whether she was right or wrong—were always interesting and always peculiarly her own. One can imagine what a contrast there was between Vera Ivanovna, with her diffuse radicalism, her subjectivity, and her turbulence, and Vladimir Ilyich. It was not that they disliked each other, but there was the feeling of deep organic incompatibility. Her psychological insight made her realize Lenin's strength, which already then she viewed with vague hostility; this showed itself in her expression about Lenin's 'deadly grip'.

Only gradually, and not without difficulty, I was becoming aware of the complexity of relationships between the members of the editorial board. As I said before, I came to London like a raw provincial in more senses than one. Not only had I never been abroad, I had never even seen Petersburg! In Moscow, just as in Kiev, I had only been in the transfer prison. I knew the Marxist authors only from their writings. In Siberia I had read a few copies of *Iskra* and also Lenin's *What is To Be Done?* I had heard about the author of *The Development of Capitalism* only in the Moscow prison (from Vanovsky, I think) as about a rising star of Social Democracy. About Martov I knew little, about Potresov, nothing. In London, reading with avidity *Iskra*, *Zaria*, and

all our other publications, I came across, in *Zaria*, a brilliant
article, on the role and significance of trade unions, directed
against Prokopovich. "Who is this Molotov?", I asked
Martov. "That is Parvus." I knew nothing about Parvus
either. I accepted *Iskra* as an entity, and during these months
it did not occur to me, (I even had an inner reluctance), to
look for differences of views, tendencies, for opposing influ-
ences either in the paper or among the editors.

I noticed that some leading articles and *feuilletons* in *Iskra*,
although not signed, were written in the first person: "In
such-and-such an issue I said" or "as I have already written"
and so on. I inquired who was the author of these pieces. It
turned out that it was Lenin. I remarked that there was
some literary awkwardness in using the first person singular
in an unsigned article.

"Why do you think so?", asked Lenin intrigued, believing, perhaps, that my remark was not quite casual, or that I
expressed more than a personal opinion.

"I don't know, but it seems so to me," I answered vaguely
because I had nothing more precise to say on this matter.

"I do not think so," Lenin chuckled enigmatically.

At that time one might have perceived a trace of 'ego-
centricity' in this literary form. However, by giving to his
articles, even the unsigned ones, a specific style, Lenin took
full personal responsibility for their political line; evidently
he was not quite sure that this line was shared by his close
collaborators. Here we had, on a small scale, the persistence,
the stubbornness of Lenin: his whole being was geared to
one great purpose and he would make use of any circumstance and disregard all formalities in straining towards his
goal—this was indeed Lenin the leader.

Iskra was under Lenin's political direction; the main con-
tributor was, however, Martov. He wrote with ease, and
interminably; just the way he talked. Lenin used to spend a
great deal of time on theoretical studies in the British
Museum. One day in the Library, he was writing a polemical
article against Nadezhdin, who at that time stood politically

somewhere between the Social Democrats and the Social Revolutionaries, and had his own little publication in Switzerland. Already, the night before, Martov (who usually worked at night) had managed to write his own long contribution about Nadezhdin.

"Have you read Julius's article on Nadezhdin?", asked Lenin when I met him at the Museum.

"Yes", I answered.

"What do you think of it?"

"It seems good."

"Well", said Lenin, "Maybe it is good, but it is not precise enough. He does not draw the conclusions. I have drafted something here," and he handed me a small sheet of paper covered with his handwriting in pencil, "and now I do not know what to do: should I add this as supplementary remarks to Julius's article?"

The next issue of *Iskra* carried Martov's article with notes by Lenin at the bottom of the page. Both the article and the notes were unsigned. I do not know whether these notes are included in Lenin's collected *Works*, but I can vouch for their authorship.

A few months later and some weeks before the Congress a sharp disagreement flared up between Lenin and Martov on the attitude to be taken towards street demonstrations, or, to be more precise, on the armed struggle with the police. Lenin maintained that it was necessary to form small armed groups so that militant workers should learn how to fight the police. Martov disagreed. The dispute came before the editors. "Would not this give rise to something like group terrorism?", was my comment on Lenin's point of view. (One should remember that at that time we were very much against the terrorist tactics of the Social Revolutionaries.) Martov took up the question and started developing the idea that one should teach the demonstrators to defend themselves against attacks by the police, but not to organize groups which would fight them. Plekhanov, towards whom I and probably others too, looked expectantly, refrained from speaking; he proposed that Martov should write down a draft of a resolution so that we could discuss the controversial issue, text in hand. However, the whole question was lost in the mass of other events and problems connected with the Congress.

I had very few occasions to observe Lenin and Martov in private, outside our conferences and meetings. Even then Lenin disliked those long palavers, formless debates and interminable chaotic conversations which inevitably led to émigré gossip and empty chatter. Martov, however, was inclined to this kind of pastime. Lenin, this most powerful 'engineer of revolution', had only one goal before his eyes, and towards this final goal he was pressing, whether in politics or in his theoretical or philosophical studies, in discussions with others or in learning foreign languages. His was perhaps the most determined utilitarianism ever produced in the laboratory of history. But as this utilitarianism was harnessed to a grand design it did not diminish or impoverish Lenin's personality—on the contrary, with the growth of experience and with the ever-widening scale of action, his personality was constantly developing and expanding.

Side by side with Lenin, Martov, his closest companion-in-arms, was already beginning to feel ill at ease. They still addressed each other in the familiar second person singular, but a certain coolness was creeping into their relations. Martov lived much more in the present with day-to-day vexations, day-to-day literary and journalistic affairs, day-to-day news, polemics and conversations. Lenin, although firmly entrenched in the present, was always trying to pierce the veil of the future. Martov evolved innumerable and often brilliant guesses, hypotheses, and propositions, which he himself promptly forgot; whereas Lenin waited and developed his when he needed them. The elaborate subtlety of Martov's ideas made Lenin anxiously shake his head. At that time the difference in their political thinking was not yet defined. Indeed, it was hardly perceptible. Only in retrospect does it seem visible. Later on, during the split at the Second

Congress, the collaborators of *Iskra* became divided into the 'hard' and the 'soft'. We know that this terminology was very much used at that time, precisely because the lines of division were not yet rigid; there were, rather, differences in approach to certain problems and in the degree of determination to go on to the very end.

As to the differences between Lenin and Martov, one can say that even before the split, before the Congress, Lenin was 'hard' and Martov 'soft'. And they both knew it. Lenin would glance at Martov, whom he highly esteemed, with a critical and somewhat suspicious look; and Martov, feeling this glance, would grow uneasy and his thin shoulders would twitch nervously. When they met and talked afterwards, at least in my presence, one missed the friendly inflection of the voice and the jests. Lenin would look beyond Martov as he talked, while Martov's eyes would grow glassy under his drooping spectacles that were never cleaned. And when Lenin spoke with me about Martov, his voice had a peculiar tone: "Oh, I see. Julius said so?"—and the name Julius was pronounced in a special way, with a slight emphasis, as if to give a warning: "Yes, yes, a good man, even a remarkable one, but very, very soft."

Undoubtedly Vera Ivanovna also had a certain influence on Martov—not a political but a psychological one; and she kept him at a distance from Lenin. Of course, all I am saying here is more of a psychological characterization than a statement of facts, and it concerns the situation as I saw it over twenty-two years ago. During these years many events impressed themselves on my memory and I may be committing an error here and there in relating these vague sentiments on personal relationships. How much do we remember and what part does our imagination—unintentionally—play in reconstructing the past? I think that in essentials I do remember what happened and how it happened.

After my, as it were, 'trial appearances' in Whitechapel (Alexeev used to give a 'report' to the members of the editorial board), I was sent on a lecture tour to Brussels, to

Liège, and to Paris. My subject was, "What is historical materialism and how do the revolutionary socialists understand it?" Vladimir Ilyich found this subject of great interest, and he looked through my plan of the lecture, my notes and quotations. He suggested that I should work over it and prepare it for publication in *Zaria*; but I never had the courage to do this.

From Paris I was recalled by telegram to London. There was talk of sending me into Russia illegally. Vladimir Ilyich thought this would be useful; comrades in Russia complained of bad organization, of lack of personnel, and I think that Clair-Kzhizhanovsky also asked for my return. But even before I reached London the plan was changed. L. G. Deutsch, who lived then in London and was always very friendly towards me, told me later how he intervened 'in my favour', maintaining that 'the youngster' (he never called me anything else) should be allowed to stay abroad in order to study. After some opposition, Lenin agreed with him. To work in the Russian organization of *Iskra* was a very tempting proposal; however, I was quite pleased to remain abroad for some time.

One Sunday I went with Vladimir Ilyich and Nadezhda Konstantinovna to a socialist church; a social democratic gathering there was accompanied by singing of pious revolutionary psalms. The main speaker was a compositor who had returned from Australia, if I am not mistaken. Vladimir Ilyich, in a whisper, was translating for our benefit his speech, which at that time, at least, sounded quite revolutionary. Then everybody stood up and sang, "Almighty God, put an end to all kings and all rich men . . ." or something to that effect. "The English proletariat has in itself many revolutionary and socialist elements", said Lenin as we left the church, "but they are all mixed up with conservatism, with religion and prejudices; and there seems to be no way in which these elements can come to the top."

It may be of interest to note that Vera Zasulich and Martov lived without any contact whatsoever with the English working-class movement; *Iskra* and all that happened around it absorbed them completely. Whereas Lenin, at least from time to time, made some independent reconnoitring into the state of that movement.

There is no need to say that Vladimir Ilyich, Nadezhda Konstantinovna, and her mother lived extremely simply. On our return from the social democratic church we had lunch in the small kitchen in their two-room flat. I remember, as if it were yesterday, the thin slices of meat served straight from the frying-pan. Then we took tea. As usual, they poked fun at me, asking whether I would be able to find my way home. Being methodical, I classified my inefficiency as 'topographical cretinism'; the streets around still remained unfamiliar to me.

The date of the Congress was approaching, and finally the decision was taken to transfer the *Iskra* centre to Geneva. Life there was incomparably cheaper; it was also easier to maintain contact from there with Russia. Very reluctantly Lenin agreed. I went first to Paris, and from there together with Martov we arrived in Geneva. The work preparatory to the Congress became more intense. Soon Lenin also came to Paris. He was to give three lectures on the agrarian problems at the so-called High School which was set up in Paris by university professors exiled from Russia. A group of Marxist students insisted on inviting Lenin after a lecture had been given by Chernov. The professors were not a little worried and asked the militant lecturer not to indulge in any polemics. Lenin, however, did not feel bound by any conditions and began his first lecture by stating that Marxism being a revolutionary theory was *ipso facto* highly controversial but that this in no way detracted from its scientific character.

Before the first lecture, I remember, Vladimir Ilyich was very nervous. But once on the rostrum he became quite composed, at least outwardly. Professor Gambarov, who came to listen, summed up his impressions to Deutsch: "A real professor!" The kind man meant in this way to pay the highest tribute to Lenin. The lectures were full of polemics against the Narodniks and against the agrarian social reformism of David, whom Lenin compared and put on the same level; and yet throughout the speaker remained within the bounds of economic theory, mentioning neither the current political struggle nor the agrarian programme of the Social Democrats nor that of the Social Revolutionaries.

These were the limits which Lenin imposed on himself in view of the academic character of his audience. But after the third lecture he made a political speech on the subject of agrarian reform, not at the High School but at 110 rue Choisy (if I remember correctly), at a meeting organized by the French group of *Iskra*. The hall was crowded. All the students from the High School came to hear the practical conclusions drawn from the theoretical exposition to which they had been treated at the School. Under discussion was the agrarian programme of *Iskra* and, in particular, the problem of the restitution of the 'cut off lands'. I do not remember who spoke as Lenin's opponent; but I do remember that Lenin was excellent in his conclusions. One of the French *Iskra* men said to me when we were leaving the hall: "Lenin surpassed himself tonight". After the meeting the organizers, of course, took the lecturer to a café. All were delighted and the lecturer himself pleasantly excited. The treasurer, very gratified, announced the receipts from the sale of entrance tickets: *Iskra* made something like 75 or 100 francs from the lecture—a sum not to be despised. All this was at the beginning of 1903. I cannot give a more precise date, but this should not be too difficult to establish—it may have been established already.

During this visit to Paris it was decided that Lenin should see an opera. N. I. Sedova, a member of the *Iskra* group, was to organize the evening. Lenin carried with him the briefcase which he took to the High School. The performance consisted of *Louisa* by Massenet (?),[8] an opera with a more

---

[8] *Louisa* was actually by Gustave Charpentier. (Translator's note.)

or less democratic theme. We all sat together in the gallery. Apart from Lenin, Sedova, and myself, there were also Martov and others whose names I do not remember.

There is connected with this visit to the Opéra Comique a little incident which has nothing to do with music. Lenin bought himself in Paris a pair of shoes which proved to be too tight. He suffered for a few hours and finally decided to get rid of them. It so happened that my own shoes were in a very poor state and Lenin gave me his new pair which at the beginning seemed to fit me quite well, and I decided to wear them on the outing to the opera. On the way there everything went smoothly. But in the opera I began to feel very uncomfortable. This was probably the reason why I remember neither my own nor Lenin's impressions of the performance; but I do remember that Lenin was in a good mood, jesting and laughing. On our way back my suffering became intolerable, with Vladimir Ilyich cruelly amusing himself at my expense. There was, however, some compassion underneath his laughter: didn't he also have a few hours of discomfort in the very same shoes?

I had mentioned Lenin's nervousness before his lectures in Paris; I feel I have to return to this remark. Lenin experienced this kind of nervousness before public appearances even later, and the less congenial the audience, the more formal the occasion, the greater would be his agitation. As a speaker, Lenin always seemed full of self-confidence; he spoke with energy and so fast that the stenographers had a hard job to keep up with him. But when he was ill at ease, his voice seemed not his own and sounded like an echo, impersonal and coming from afar. However, when he felt that *this* particular audience was really in need of learning just what *he* had to say, his voice acquired all its vivacity, flexibility, and persuasiveness, not of the 'oratorical' kind, but a conversational one, adapted to the needs of the rostrum. There was no art of oratory in Lenin's speeches, yet his was more than uncommon eloquence. One may, of course, say that every speaker addresses the audience he feels to be *his* with more ease and success; this is perfectly true. The question arises, however, what circumstances and what audience make the speaker feel himself among *his* listeners. European orators of the type of a Vanderwelde, brought up in the parliamentary tradition, need a certain degree of solemnity and a formal atmosphere in order to achieve an effect. They feel most relaxed at formal or official celebrations. For Lenin any such gathering was a minor disaster. His most brilliant and convincing speeches were those in which he analysed the problems of political struggle: he was probably at his best when addressing the members of the Central Committee on the eve of October.

Before his lectures in Paris, I think I only heard Lenin once in London at the end of December 1902. It is strange that I have no recollection either of the occasion or of the subject matter of the speech. I even seem to doubt: was it really Lenin who spoke then? But, yes, surely; a large meeting of Russians in London was an important event. Lenin would not have been there if he was not going to address it. The only way I can explain this lapse of memory is the following: in all probability Lenin devoted his lecture to the same subject which was discussed in the leading article of the current copy of *Iskra*. By that time I had already been able to read Lenin's article, so that his speech had nothing new for me. After the lecture there was no debate. Among the 'Londoners' there were no opponents confident enough to contradict Lenin. Part of the audience consisted of anarchists and part of the members of the *Bund*; as the atmosphere was not very gratifying, the whole occasion vanished without leaving any impression. I only remember that at the end of the meeting I was approached by the couple B. who had belonged to the former Petersburg group of *Rabochaya Mysl* (*Workers' Thought*) and had lived for quite a time in London. "Come to us on New Year's eve", they said (this is why I remember that the meeting took place at the end of December). "What for?", I asked like a real barbarian. "Well, we shall spend the evening in a circle of comrades. Ulyanov will come, and Krupskaya will be there." I remember that they said 'Ulyanov' and not Lenin, so that at first I did not realize about whom they were talking. It turned out that Vera Zasulich and Martov were also invited. Next day in 'the den' we deliberated what to do; then we inquired whether Lenin was going. In the end, I think, nobody went. This was a pity; it would have been a unique opportunity to see Lenin with Zasulich and Martov in the atmosphere of a New Year's party.

After my arrival in Geneva from Paris I was invited, together with Zasulich and Martov, to Plekhanov; I think Vladimir Ilyich came too. Of that evening I have a very blurred recollection. In any case, it was not a political gathering, but a 'social', not to say a philistine one. I remember that I sat there rather helpless and bored; from time to time the host or the hostess gave me some attention, otherwise I did not know what to do with myself. Plekhanov's daughters were serving tea and cakes; there was some tension in the air and probably I was not the only one to feel ill at ease. Or perhaps I felt the coolness much more sharply because I was so much younger? This was my first and last visit there and, of course, my impressions were fleeting and perhaps also casual, as casual and fleeting as were all my encounters with Plekhanov. I have tried to give a brief impression of that brilliant Marxist teacher and the foremost master of Marxism in Russia, elsewhere; here I want simply to convey my impressions of the first contacts in which, alas, I was not very fortunate. Zasulich, worried by this unhappy state of affairs, used to say: "I know that George can be impossible but, really, he is quite a nice animal." (This was her favourite eulogy.)

I should like to mention here that in the home of the Axelrods the atmosphere was one of simplicity and sincere comradeship. To this day I remember with gratitude the hours I spent at the Axelrods' hospitable family table during my frequent trips to Zürich. Vladimir Ilyich spent much time there too, and to judge from the way the Axelrods spoke about his visits, he must have appreciated their warmth and cordiality. It so happened that I never met Lenin in Axelrod's home.

Vera Zasulich's attitude towards young comrades, her simplicity and friendliness, were quite exceptional. If one could not speak of her 'hospitality' it was only because she was more in need of it herself than she ever could offer. She lived, ate, and dressed like the most modest of students. Of material goods her only passions were tobacco and mustard—consuming both in huge quantities. When she covered the thinnest slice of ham with a thick layer of mustard, we used to say: "Vera Ivanovna is feasting".

L. G. Deutsch, the fourth member of the group of *Emancipation of Labour*, was also remarkably kind and attentive towards the young. So far I have failed to mention that as the manager of *Iskra* Deutsch took part in the editorial meetings in which he had a consultative voice. He usually followed Plekhanov and his views in the matter of revolutionary tactics were more than moderate. One day, to my utter amazement, he declared:

"There won't be any armed uprising, young man, and there is no need for it. In deportation we also had those pugnacious cocks who at the slightest provocation went into battle and were destroyed. My attitude was different: to stand firm, to make the administration understand that it might come to a big battle, but never to get involved. In this way I gained both the respect of the administration and the softening of the regime. We should adopt the same tactics towards Tsarism, otherwise we shall be beaten and destroyed without any advantage to the cause."

This tactical prognostication was so stupefying that I repeated it to Martov and to Zasulich and to Lenin. I have forgotten Martov's reaction, but Vera Ivanovna said: "Eugene" (this was Deutsch's old pseudonym) "was always like that: personally a man of exceptional courage, but politically extremely prudent and moderate." Lenin listened to me, then muttered something like "Hm . . . Hm . . .

Yea", and we both burst out laughing without expressing any opinion.

The delegates to the Second Congress began arriving in Geneva and we went into an unending series of meetings. In this preparatory work Lenin indisputably—though not always obviously—played the leading role. There were meetings of the *Iskra* editorial board, and meetings of the *Iskra* organization; separate meetings with groups of delegates and separate plenary sessions. Some delegates were full of doubts or reservations, or brought with them complaints or grievances. These preliminaries absorbed a great deal of time.

Only three workers came to take part in the Congress. Lenin entered into long discussions with each of them, and won them over. One was Shotman from Petersburg. He was still a very young man, but sensible and thoughtful. After one of his talks with Lenin he came back—we stayed in the same lodgings—and kept on repeating, "And how his small eyes were sparkling—one would think he can see through. . . ."

The delegate from Nikolaev was Kalafati. Vladimir Ilyich questioned me about him in great detail as I had known him at Nikolaev, and then, smiling slyly, remarked: "He said he knew you when you were something of a Tolstoyan".

"Oh, what nonsense", I answered, almost indignant.

"Well, what's wrong with that?" said Lenin half-teasing and half-reassuring, "you were then about eighteen years old and, you know, people are not born Marxists."

"Yes, that's true, but I certainly had nothing in common with Tolstoyanism."

In the preliminary discussions a great deal of attention was given to the formulation of the statutes; and the most important problem was that of the structure of the organization, which was to determine the relations between its central journal and its Central Committee. I had come abroad with the idea that the 'central organ', that is the journal, should be 'subordinated' to the Central Committee. The majority of the *Iskra* men in Russia held this view too, though neither very clearly nor in a very determined manner.

"This will not work," Lenin insisted, "because of the relation of forces. . . Well, how will they direct us from inside Russia? No, it won't work. . . We constitute the stable centre and we shall direct affairs from here."

One of the resolutions demanded that the 'central organ' should undertake to publish articles written by members of the Central Committee.

"Even those articles which go against the 'central organ'?" asked Lenin.

"Of course."

"What for? This will not do. A controversy among two members of the 'central organ' might in certain circumstances be of some use, but a polemic of the Central Committee members who are in Russia against the 'central organ' outside Russia is unacceptable."

"In that case the 'central organ' will exercise a complete dictatorship?" I asked.

"What's wrong with that?", retorted Lenin, "In our present situation it cannot be otherwise."

A great deal of confusion was caused by the so-called 'right of co-optation'. At one of the meetings we, that is the young ones, reached the decision that there should be a right of 'positive co-optation' and of 'negative co-optation'.

"But what you call 'negative co-optation' means in good Russian the right to chuck someone out", laughed Vladimir Ilyich next morning. "It is not so simple. Well, you just try to apply—ha! ha! ha!—your 'right of negative co-optation' to the editorial board of *Iskra*!"

For Lenin the most important problem was how to organize the 'central organ' (that is *Iskra*) in such a way that in practice it should play the role of the Central Committee as well. In his view it was impossible to preserve the old team of 'the six'. On all controversial questions Zasulich and Axelrod almost invariably sided with Plekhanov, so at best there resulted a stalemate of three votes against three;

and neither of them would ever agree to the exclusion of anybody from the board. The only way out which remained was its enlargement. Lenin intended to include me in the editorial team and then within it to create a smaller body of three editors: Plekhanov, Martov, and himself. Vladimir Ilyich was initiating me into his plan gradually; moreover, he did not even mention to me that he had already proposed my candidature as the seventh member of the team and that this was accepted by everybody except Plekhanov, who opposed the whole plan with great determination. In his opinion, the admission of the seventh member automatically prejudiced the chances of the *Emancipation of Labour* group; there would be four 'young' members against three 'old' ones.

I think that all this was the main reason for Plekhanov's obviously unfriendly attitude towards me. In addition, as ill-luck would have it, there arose between us some disagreements which became only too plain to the delegates. First, if I am not mistaken, there was the project to set up a popular newspaper. Some delegates insisted on the need to create, besides *Iskra*, a popular journal which would, if possible, be published in Russia. This was in particular the project of the *Southern Worker* group, a project to which Lenin was decidedly opposed. His objections were many and varied, but the main one was the fear that a new grouping could form itself on the basis of 'popular', simplified principles of social democracy before the kernel of the party proper became solid and well established. Plekhanov declared himself for the creation of a popular paper, firmly opposing Lenin's point of view and openly seeking the support of regional delegates. I was on Lenin's side.

At one of the meetings I argued—whether correctly or not it does not matter now—that what we needed was not a popular newspaper, but a series of propagandist pamphlets and booklets which would help the advanced workers to rise to the level of articles in *Iskra*; that a popular publication would narrow the scope of *Iskra* and would blur the political physiognomy of the party, pushing it down to the level of 'Economism' and 'Eserism'.[9] Plekhanov objected. "Why should it blur the physiognomy of the party? Of course," he went on, "in a popular periodical we shall not be able to express everything; we shall raise certain demands, put forward certain slogans, but we shall not debate tactical problems there. We shall tell the worker that one must fight against capitalism, but obviously we shall not enter into a theoretical discussion about *how* one should fight against capitalism."

I seized upon this argument: "But the SRs and those who preach economism also say that one should fight against capitalism. We disagree with them precisely on the point of *how* to fight. If in a popular paper we do not answer this very question, we immediately blur the difference between ourselves and the SRs." My reasoning seemed convincing and Plekhanov found no answer to it. This incident did not, of course, improve his attitude towards me. Soon we had another conflict—this time at the editorial meeting. It was decided that before the whole question of the staff of *Iskra* was finally settled by the Congress, I should participate in the meetings, without voting rights. Plekhanov categorically objected to this. Vera Ivanovna declared, "Yet, I shall bring him along." And indeed, she did "bring me along".

What went on behind the scenes I learned only much later; I appeared at the meeting knowing nothing and quite unconcerned. Plekhanov greeted me with the studious coolness of which he was a past master. It so happened that at this particular meeting the editors had to occupy themselves with the conflict which arose between Deutsch and Blumenfeld, whom I have already mentioned. Deutsch was the manager of *Iskra*. Blumenfeld was in charge of the printing shop. Blumenfeld resented Deutsch's interference in the internal affairs of the printing shop. Plekhanov, in the name of old friendship, supported Deutsch and proposed that

---

[9] SRs—members of the Social Revolutionary Party.

Blumenfeld should deal exclusively with the business of printing. I maintained that one cannot run a printing shop on that basis; apart from the process and techniques of printing there were also administrative and organizational questions and that in these Blumenfeld should be given a free hand. I remember the venom with which Plekhanov retorted: "No doubt Comrade Trotsky is right, in so far as on the basis of technique there arise various superstructures —administrative and others—this is exactly what the theory of historical materialism teaches us; however . . ." and so on, and so on.

Lenin and Martov cautiously supported me and the appropriate resolution was accepted. But this was the last straw . . . In both incidents, as we have seen, Lenin took my side. But at the same time he observed anxiously how my relations with Plekhanov were deteriorating. This was finally threatening his whole plan of the reorganization of the editorial board. At one of the next meetings with the newly-arrived delegates, Lenin took me aside and said: "About the popular paper, leave Martov to oppose Plekhanov. Martov will muddle up the whole affair, while you will hammer at it. It's better to let it lapse. . . ." These expressions, "muddle up" and "hammer" I remember clearly.

After one editorial session which took place in the Café Landolt, or perhaps after the session mentioned above, Zasulich, in a manner so characteristic of her, timidly yet insistently complained that we were attacking the liberals "too much". This was her sore point. "But look, they are trying hard," she said looking past Lenin though she was addressing herself to Lenin primarily. "In the last copy of *The Emancipation*, Struve offers the example of Jaurès and calls upon Russian liberals not to break with socialism, otherwise they will be threatened with the pitiful fate of German liberalism. They should instead take their cue from French radical-socialists."

Lenin stood at the table, his imitation Panama hat on his

head (the session was practically finished and he was about to leave).

"One more reason to attack them strongly", he said, smiling gaily and as if teasing Vera Ivanovna.

"Well . . . Well . . !" she exclaimed despairingly, "they make a step in our direction, and we have to 'attack them strongly'."

"That's right. Struve tells his liberals: against our socialism one should not behave in that coarse German fashion, but rather with French *finesse*: one should attract, bribe, deceive, corrupt in the manner of French radicals of the left who are flirting with Jaurèsism."

I do not, of course, relate this memorable conversation word for word. But the sense of it and the atmosphere remain extremely vivid in my memory. At the moment I have not at hand any material which would allow me to check the facts, but this should be quite easy. It is enough to look through the copies of *The Emancipation* from the spring of 1903 and find Struve's article dealing with the attitude of liberals towards democratic socialism in general and towards Jaurèsism in particular. This article I remember precisely in connection with Vera Zasulich's words and with the incident described here. If, looking at the date of *The Emancipation*, one adds the time needed for the paper to reach Geneva, and for Vera Zasulich to read it—that is, two, three or four days—one can with enough exactitude arrive at the date of the altercation in the Café Landolt. It was, I recollect, a spring-like day (it might have been early summer), the sun was shining brightly and Lenin was smiling good-humouredly. I remember his quietly mocking voice, his self-confidence and his 'solid' figure—yes, he looked 'solid', though he was then much thinner than in the last years of his life. Vera Ivanovna was, as usual, fidgety, turning this way and that; nobody, it seems, intervened in this conversation which, in any case, lasted no longer than the time taken in getting ready to leave. I returned home together with Vera Ivanovna. She was depressed, feeling that Struve was beaten at his game. I could offer no consolation. None of us, however, foresaw at that time to what degree, how definitely, all the aces of Russian liberalism were trumped in that little dialogue at the entrance to the Café Landolt.

I realize the inadequacy of all I have so far narrated. My story sounds poorer than I had imagined when I started on it. But I assembled carefully all that my memory retained, even episodes of little significance, because there is hardly any one now who can describe this period in greater detail. Plekhanov is dead. Zasulich is dead. Martov is dead. And Lenin is dead. It is doubtful that any one of them have left memoirs. Perhaps Vera Ivanovna? But we have heard nothing about it. Of the old editorial team only Axelrod and Potresov are left. But, apart from all other considerations, they both took a small part in the editorial work and were only rarely present at the editorial meetings. Deutsch would perhaps have something more to say, but he came abroad only shortly before my arrival, towards the end of the period I have been describing; besides, he was little involved directly in the work of the editorial board.

Invaluable information could be provided, and let us hope will be provided, by Nadezhda Konstantinovna. At that time she was in the centre of all organizational activity. It was to her that newly arrived comrades reported first; she briefed those who were leaving and sent them on their way; she established contacts and clandestine connections; she gave instructions, wrote letters, coded and decoded notices and messages. Nearly always her room held that faint smell of paper warmed up over a flame. And how often did she complain with her soft insistence that people did not write enough, or that someone made mistakes in the code, or wrote in chemical ink in such a way that one line was blurred by the next, and so on. Even more important, of course, was the fact that in this organizational work at Lenin's side she could observe day after day all that occurred

to him and around him. Nonetheless, I hope that my remarks will not prove valueless, especially as Nadezhda
Konstantinovna was very rarely present at our staff meetings,
at least during my time; but mainly also because it may
happen that the fresh eye of an outsider notices what more
familiar eyes might miss. Be that as it may, what I have
narrated I have narrated.

And now I should like to make a few general remarks:
I am chiefly interested in explaining why, in my view, Lenin
should have undergone that decisive crisis of his political
personality precisely during the period of the old *Iskra*, of
his, so to speak, political self-evaluation; why this crisis was
both inevitable and necessary.

Lenin went abroad a fully mature man of thirty. In Russia,
in the circle of students, in the first social democratic groupings, in the colonies of deportees, his was the leading role.
He could not be unaware of his strength, if only because it
was acknowledged by all those who met him and by all
those who worked with him. He had left Russia with a
considerable theoretical knowledge and with a great deal of
political experience—all this was permeated through and
through by that powerful striving towards *the* goal so
characteristic of his mental make-up. Abroad he had to
collaborate with *The Emancipation of Labour* group and
first of all with Plekhanov, that profound and brilliant
interpreter of Marx, the theoretician, the politician, the
publicist, the orator of European fame with European connections from whom so many had learned.

Next to Plekhanov there stood two great authorities:
Zasulich and Axelrod. It was not only her heroic past that
made of Zasulich a prominent figure: it was her perspicacity,
her erudition especially in the field of history, and her exceptional psychological intuition. It was through Zasulich that
'The Group' had in the past established relations with the
old Engels. In contrast to Plekhanov and Zasulich, who had
strong links with socialism in the latin countries, Axelrod
represented the idea and the experience of German Social

Democracy. This division of 'spheres of influence' was reflected also in their places of residence: Plekhanov and Zasulich settled in Geneva, while Axelrod lived in Zürich. Axelrod concentrated on matters of tactics and, as we know, did not produce any theoretical or historical work. Generally speaking, he wrote little and in his writing he dealt nearly always with the tactical problems of socialism. Here he displayed both originality and shrewdness. From our innumerable conversations—at one time my relations with him and Zasulich were very friendly—I saw clearly that much of Plekhanov's writing on tactical questions was a product of a collective mind, and that Axelrod's contribution was much weightier than one could deduce from printed documents alone. Axelrod himself used to say to Plekhanov who (until the 1903 split) was the undisputed and beloved chief of 'The Group': "You, George, have a long trunk: you'll reach out far for whatever you may need. . . ." Axelrod, as we know, wrote a preface to Lenin's *Tasks of Russian Social Democrats*, the manuscript of which was sent out of Russia. By this act it was as though 'The Group' had adopted the young talented Russian activist, at the same time establishing the relationship of masters towards the disciple. It was precisely as a disciple that Lenin, with two other comrades, went abroad. I was not present at the first encounters of the pupil with the teachers and at those meetings at which the political line of *Iskra* was being hammered out. It is not difficult, however, in the light of events I have described, and especially in the light of the Second Party Congress, to understand that the very sharpness of the conflict, apart from the differences in principles which only just began to come to the surface, was also caused by the mistaken view the 'old' ones took of Lenin's stature and eminence.

During the Second Congress and right after it, the indignation with which Axelrod and the other members of the editorial board criticized Lenin's behaviour was mixed with perplexity. How dared he go that far? This perplexity increased further, when after the rupture between Plekhanov and Lenin—which occurred very soon after the Congress—Lenin continued the struggle. The frame of mind of Axelrod and the others might perhaps be even better conveyed by the expression, 'What on earth bit him?'. Not so long ago he left Russia, so reasoned the 'old' ones, and came here as a pupil and behaved like one (this was particularly stressed by Axelrod in what he said about the first months of *Iskra*). From whence this sudden self-confidence? How dared he? Then there were guesses. He had prepared the ground in Russia. Not for nothing were the 'lines of communication' in the hands of Nadezhda Konstantinovna. It was there that the minds of comrades were being stealthily influenced against *The Emancipation of Labour* group.

Vera Zasulich was no less indignant than the others, but perhaps better than they she understood what was happening. Not without reason did she say about Lenin, still a long time before the split, that, unlike Plekhanov's, his was a "deadly grip". And who knows what impression these words had made on Lenin at the time? Perhaps he said to himself: yes, this is true. Who understands Plekhanov better than Vera Zasulich? He shakes and shakes, and then lets go, and the task is not just to shake and let go. . . What is needed is the "deadly grip".

To what extent and in what sense it might have been true that there was some preliminary 'working over' the minds and opinions of comrades in Russia, Nadezhda Konstantinovna can tell better than anyone else. Even without knowing all the facts, one can assume that this was broadly true. Lenin was always preparing for tomorrow, while strengthening and consolidating what he had gained today. His creative thought never stood still; his vigilance never flagged. When he became convinced that *The Emancipation of Labour* group was incapable of providing the immediate leadership of the militant vanguard of the proletariat in the approaching revolution, he drew from this all the practical conclusions. The 'old' members of the organization—and not only they—were mistaken: this was no longer the young and remarkable activist, whose work Axelrod introduced by providing it with a friendly, patronizing preface, this was a leader totally geared to one purpose; and it seemed that he grew conscious of being a leader when acting side by side with his elders; together with the teachers he realized that he was stronger and more indispensable than they.

True, in Russia, according to Martov, Lenin was already *primus inter pares*. But there he still acted in narrow social-democratic circles, in newly-formed organizations. Russian party men still bore the stamp of parochialism. How many Lassalles did they have, how many Bebels? The stature of *The Emancipation of Labour* group was quite different. Plekhanov, Axelrod, and Zasulich were on a level with Kautsky, Lafargue, Guesde, and Bebel—the real German Bebel! Lenin applied the great European scale when he measured his forces against theirs. It was precisely in the disputes with Plekhanov, when the editorial board was divided into two camps, that Lenin acquired that firmness and self-confidence without which he would not have become the Lenin of the future. The disagreements with the 'old' members were unavoidable, not because there were *a priori* two conceptions of a revolutionary movement—at that time this was not so; what divided them was a different approach to political events, to practical and to organizational questions, and, in consequence, a different vision of the coming revolution. The old members had already been émigrés for twenty years. For them *Iskra* and *Zaria* were, first and foremost, literary enterprises, while for Lenin the two publications constituted an immediately valuable instrument of revolutionary action. Somewhere deep in Plekhanov was hidden the revolution's sceptic. This came to the surface later, in 1905 and 1906 and, even more tragically, during the imperialist war. He was looking down upon Lenin's characteristic concentration on the one and unique goal, and had up his sleeve quite a few condescending and malicious jokes about it.

Axelrod, as we have seen, was more preoccupied with

tactical problems, but his mind stubbornly refused to move beyond preliminaries to the preparatory. Very often Axelrod displayed considerable art in analysing tendencies and nuances which characterized particular groups of revolutionary intelligentsia. He was a homeopath of pre-revolutionary politics. He applied procedures and methods of a laboratory; he dealt with minute quantities; he observed the smallest groups; he weighed everything on a chemist's scale. Not for nothing L. G. Deutsch considered Axelrod as belonging to the same type as Spinoza. It was not without significance that Spinoza was a diamond-cutter, this job, as we know, requiring a magnifying glass. Lenin, on the contrary, saw the vast scale of events and relationships, trained his mind to reach to the depth of social masses and that enabled him to react to the approaching revolution which caught Plekhanov and Axelrod unawares.

Vera Zasulich, it seemed, felt more directly than the other old members of *Iskra* the imminence of the revolution. Her understanding of history—lively, devoid of pedantry and shot through with intuition—helped her greatly. But her vision of the revolution was that of an old radical. In the depth of her soul she was convinced that we had already all the elements of the revolution with the exception of the 'true', self-confident liberalism which should be the leading force. She was of the opinion that we, Marxists, by our untimely criticism of the liberals and by our 'baiting' of them, were really playing a counter-revolutionary role. True, she never expressed such views publicly; even in personal conversations she was rarely outspoken, but nevertheless such were her innermost thoughts. From there stemmed her antagonism to Paul Axelrod whom she considered a doctrinaire. Indeed, within the limits of his laboratory tactics he invariably insisted on the dominant role of social democracy; however he refused to transfer the application of his doctrine from groupings and circles to social classes when social classes were on the move. Here was the gulf that separated him from Lenin.

Lenin went abroad neither as a Marxist 'generally speaking', nor in order to devote himself to some 'general' literary-revolutionary work, nor for the purpose of carrying on the twenty-year-old activities of *The Emancipation of Labour*. No. He went as a potential leader, as *the* leader of the revolution which was welling up, which he sensed and perceived. He went in order to build, in the shortest possible time, an ideological base and an organizational framework for that revolution. When I spoke about Lenin's tense concentration on his goal—concentration which was both passionate and disciplined—I did not see it as an effort to achieve a 'final triumph', no, that would have been too vague and meaningless; I saw it as a concrete, direct, immediate work towards the practical aim of speeding up the outbreak of the revolution and of securing its victory.

When Lenin, in his activities abroad, found himself side by side with Plekhanov and when there was no longer between them what the Germans call "the impressiveness of distance", it became quite clear to the 'pupil' that in matters which were at that time essential, he, the pupil, not only had almost nothing to learn from the master, but the master, by his procrastination and scepticism, hindered the work which had to be done and, because of his authority, deflected from it younger collaborators. Hence Lenin's far-sighted preoccupation with the editorial team; hence his combinations of 'the seven' and 'the three'; hence the endeavour to separate Plekhanov from *The Emancipation of Labour* group, to form the leading triumvirate in which Plekhanov would still have a say on the subject of revolutionary theory and Martov on that of revolutionary politics. Personal alliances may be altered, but the bare bones of the plan for the future remained unchanged and finally were clothed with sinew, flesh, and blood.

At the Second Congress Lenin won Plekhanov over, but without hope of retaining him for long. At the same time he lost Martov, and lost him for good. Plekhanov must have sensed something during the Congress. To Axelrod, who reproached him bitterly for his amazing alliance with Lenin, he replied, "From such stuff Robespierres are made". Was this significant remark ever published? Has it ever been known in the party? Anyway, I can guarantee its authenticity. "From such stuff Robespierres are made!" "And something even greater, George Valentinovich," was history's answer. But evidently this historical discovery faded very quickly in Plekhanov's own consciousness. He broke with Lenin and returned to his scepticism and to the jokes which, incidentally, with the passage of time were losing some of their sting.

In the split, which was already casting its shadow, it was not only Plekhanov and not only the problem of the old members that played a role. The Second Congress in general marked the end of the first, preliminary stage of the preparatory period. The mere fact that the *Iskra* organization quite unexpectedly became divided into two more or less equal groupings, was in itself proof that at that stage many problems were as yet unresolved. The conception of a party based on a social class was only just dawning upon the consciousness of intellectual radicals. The flow of intelligentsia towards Marxism was still continuing. The student movement, at least its left wing, was being attracted to *Iskra*. Among intelligent young people, especially abroad, there were many groups forming themselves, which declared their support for *Iskra*. All this was still very youthful, very immature and, on the whole, rather unstable. At meetings girl students asked questions such as, "Should a girl, an adherent of *Iskra*, marry a naval officer?" Only three workers took part in the Congress, and they were brought in not without some trouble. On the one hand *Iskra* was recruiting and training professional revolutionary cadres and attracting young and idealistic workers. On the other hand, considerable numbers of intellectuals were 'passing through' *Iskra* and then transforming themselves into *Emancipators*.

Iskra was successful not only as a Marxist organ of an emerging proletarian party, but also as a highly articulate militant political journal of extreme left views. The most radical elements among the intelligentsia were, on the spur of the moment, ready to fight for liberty under the banner of *Iskra*; however, with their didactic-progressive frame of mind, they remained distrustful of the proletariat. Previously this distrust found its expression in 'economism'; later it took on, almost ingenuously, the protective colouring of *Iskra* without undergoing any fundamental change. In the final reckoning it was clear that the real conquests of *Iskra* were much less impressive than its brilliant victory. How far Lenin was aware of this fact before the Second Congress, I would not undertake to say now; but undoubtedly it was clearer and more evident to him than to anybody else. Among all these varied tendencies and attitudes assembled under the banner of *Iskra*, which found their reflection in the editorial team, Lenin was the only one to personify the future: its grave tasks, its cruel struggles and innumerable victims. Hence the vigilance and suspicion of a combatant. Hence his precision in dealing with matters of organization which found its symbolic expression in the famous Paragraph 1 (of the Statutes) determining the membership of the party. It was quite natural therefore that at the Second Congress which was getting ready to gather the fruits of the ideological victories of *Iskra*, Lenin began the task of sifting the cadres anew in a more stern and exacting manner. To take such a step facing the opposition of half the assembly, having Plekhanov as a doubtful semi-ally and all the other members of the editorial staff as determined opponents; to embark in such conditions on a work like this, one had to have faith not only in the cause but also in one's own strength.

This faith in his own strength was the result of Lenin's self-evaluation tested in practical experience. He acquired it also during the work with the 'masters' and through the first skirmishes—already then there were sparks flying and flashes of lightning portending the thunders and the tempests of the coming rupture. It was Lenin's impressive singleness of purpose which allowed him to embark upon his task and to conclude it. Tirelessly, he was tightening the string of his bow more and more, to the limit—quietly testing: was there no flaw? no danger that it would snap? From all sides he heard warnings: do not make it any tauter, don't!

"It will not snap," answered the master archer, "our bow is made of unbreakable proletarian stuff, and the string has to be tightened more and more, for the arrow is heavy and we have to launch it far, very far into the distance."

March 5th 1924.

2

On the Eve

A T AMHERST, in the Canadian prisoners of war camp,
I learned from American newspapers that Lenin had
returned to Petersburg and was addressing meetings
of workers, attacking the war and the Provisional Government. The German sailors, interned together with me, were
greatly interested in Lenin, whose name they met now for
the first time in press dispatches. My fellow internees looked
forward with great impatience to the end of hostilities which
would open the gates of their prison. They listened with
considerable attention to any voice raised against the war.
Up to now they had heard only about Liebknecht, but they
had always been told that he sold himself to the enemy. Now
they came across Lenin's name. Soon I was telling them
about what had happened in Zimmerwald and at Kienthal;
Lenin's anti-war activity made many of them recall the
ideas of Liebknecht.

Passing through Finland I first got hold of recent Russian
newspapers. They announced that Tseretelli, Skobelev, and
other 'socialists' had entered the Provisional Government.
This made the situation absolutely clear. On the second or
third day after I reached Petersburg I read Lenin's 'April
Theses'. This was just what the revolution was in need of.
Only later did I see his article 'First State of the First
Revolution', in *Pravda*, which had still been sent from
Switzerland.

The old pre-revolutionary copies of Pravda should be
re-read even now, for they are extremely interesting and
politically illuminating. Against a great deal of confused

writing, Lenin's 'Letters from Afar' stand out in all their intensity and concentration. His dispassionate theoretical exposition brings to mind a powerful, tightly wound up coil of steel later to unwind, expand, and encompass the whole ideology of the revolution.

I arranged with Comrade Kamenev to meet the editors of *Pravda* a few days after my return. I think I went to see them on May 5th or 6th. I told Lenin that I was in complete agreement with his 'April Theses' and with the whole course which the party had taken since his arrival, and that I saw before me two possibilities: either to join the party of my own—'individually'—or to attempt to bring into it the best of the 'Unionists', among whom in Petersburg alone there were 3000 workers and allied with them a whole *Pléiade* of inestimable revolutionaries like Uritsky, Lunacharsky, Yoffe, Vladimirov, Manuilsky, Karakhan, Yureniev, Posern, Litkens, and others.[1]

At that time Antonov-Ovseenko had already joined the party; so had Sokolnikov if I am not mistaken. Lenin categorically declared himself for neither solution: first of all one had to acquire a more concrete knowledge of the situation and of the people involved. He did not exclude the possibility of cooperation with Martov, and, generally speaking, with some of the Mensheviks-internationalists who had just returned from abroad; one also had to find out what the collaboration of the 'internationalists' would look like in practice.

Having met with Lenin's tacit and general approval, I personally refrained from forcing the course of events. We had a common policy. From the very first day of my arrival in Petersburg when I addressed soldiers' meetings, I used the expression 'We, Bolsheviks and internationalists'. As the 'and' proved only to hinder the flow of my arguments, I dropped it and shortened the sentence: 'We, Bolsheviks-

---

[1] Trotsky speaks here about the Inter-Borough Organization, the *Mezhrayonka*, of which he was the leader. (Translator's note.)

internationalists'. In such a way our political union pre-
ceeded the organizational one.[2]

Before the July Days, I visited the editorial offices of
Pravda perhaps twice or three times—always at some very
critical juncture.[3] During those first meetings, and even
more so after the July Days, Lenin invariably seemed
extremely preoccupied—under the apparent calmness and
his usual matter-of-fact behaviour one could sense a tremendous inner tension. At that time the Kerensky regime
seemed all-powerful. Bolshevism seemed a *quantité néglige-
able*. The party itself was not yet aware of its gathering
strength. And yet Lenin was leading it, unfalteringly, towards momentous tasks. . .

His speeches at the First Congress of the Soviets surprised
the Social Revolutionary and the Menshevik majority and
provoked their anxiety. Confused, they sensed that this man
was aiming very, very high. But they did not see his goal.
And the petty-bourgeois revolutionaries wondered: What is
he? Who is he? Simply a madman or a historical missile
endowed with an unheard of explosive force?

Lenin's address to the Congress of the Soviets, in which
he spoke about the necessity of arresting fifty capitalists, was
not perhaps quite a success from an oratorical point of view.
Yet it was of exceptional significance. The short applause of
the few Bolsheviks present accompanied the speaker leaving
the rostrum: he made the impression of someone who had
not as yet said all he had to say, or who said it not quite as
he wished to. . . At that moment an extraordinary breath of
air drifted over the hall: it was the blast of the wind of
future change felt by everybody, while bewildered eyes
anxiously followed Lenin's figure, so ordinary and so
enigmatic.

---

[2] N. N. Sukhanov in *The Russian Revolution—1917* construes my
line as differing from that of Lenin. But then Sukhanov is known as
a 'constructivist'.

[3] July Days—premature, spontaneous and abortive semi-insurrection
after which severe reprisals followed. (Translator's note.)

What is this? Who is he? Had not Plekhanov described, in his own paper, Lenin's first speech in revolutionary Petersburg as sheer folly? Was it not clear that the delegates with a mandate from the people were, nearly all of them, joining either the Social Revolutionaries or the Mensheviks? And at times even among the Bolsheviks had not Lenin's position provoked violent disagreement?

On the one hand Lenin demanded a definite break not only with bourgeois liberalism, but also with the partisans of 'national defence' no matter what their political complexion. He organized a struggle within his own party against those 'old Bolsheviks' who, as he wrote, "have more than once played so grievous a role in the history of our party by repeating a formula meaninglessly *learned by rote*, instead of *studying* the specific and new features of actual reality."[4] In this way, it might have seemed that he was weakening his own party. At the same time he declared at the Congress of the Soviets: "It is not true to say that no party exists which is ready to assume power; such a party exists: this is our party." Was there not an enormous contradiction between the position of a 'circle of propagandists' who kept their distance from all other groups and this haughty claim to assume power over this vast country shaken to its very foundations? And the Congress of the Soviets was absolutely unable to comprehend what he did want and what he hoped for, this strange man, this cool visionary, who wrote short articles in a small newspaper.

When Lenin, with superb sincerity, which only simpletons took for simple-mindedness, declared: "Our party is ready to assume power", there was laughter in the hall. "You can laugh as much as you like", said Lenin. He knew that "he laughs best who laughs last". The French saying appealed to Lenin because he was getting ready to have the last laugh himself. And in a quiet manner he went on proving that, to

---

[4] Lenin, *Selected Works*, vol. VI, p. 33, Moscow–London, 1934–37. (Translator's note.)

start with, fifty or a hundred more important millionaires should be arrested; that people should be told that we consider all capitalists to be robbers and that Tereshchenko was only less clever but in no way better than Miliukov. All these were such terribly, such abominably, naïve ideas! And this representative of a small section of the Soviets, which from time to time gave him little applause, declared: "Are you afraid of taking power? Well, we are prepared to take it." In response, there was, of course, laughter, indulgent and condescending laughter, with just a shade of alarm in it.

Furthermore, as the text of his second speech Lenin chose some extremely plain words from a letter of a peasant: how one should exert more pressure on the bourgeoisie so that it "bursts at the seams", because only then would the war finish, and if we did not exert that pressure, things would go badly. Did this simple, naïve quotation constitute Lenin's whole programme? How was one not to remain bewildered? Again some laughter, indulgent and anxious. And indeed, if one were to consider this as a programme of a propagandist group, the words "to exert pressure on the bourgeoisie" would not have much weight in themselves. And yet those who at the time were so baffled by Lenin's speech did not realize that he was unerringly interpreting history's growing pressure on the bourgeoisie which would in the end inexorably "burst at the seams". Not without reason had Lenin, last May, explained to Maklakov that "the country of workers and poor peasants was a thousand times more to the left than the Chernovs and the Tseretellis, and a hundred times more to the left than all of us, Bolsheviks."

Here was the main source of Lenin's tactics. Through the new but already crumbling democratic surface of things, he was looking deep down into "the country of workers and peasants" ready for the great revolution, with that readiness which it was still impossible to express in political terms. Every political party, which spoke in the name of the workers and peasants, was cheating them. Millions of workers and peasants did not yet know our party, had as yet to find out that it was precisely our party which stood for all they were striving for; on the other hand our party was not yet aware of its own potential strength and for this reason it was "a hundred times" more to the right than were the workers and the peasants. What was needed was a two-way traffic: the masses had to discover our party; the party in its turn had to discover the masses. One had to beware of running too much in advance; one had to beware of lagging behind; the task was to enlighten patiently and with perseverance; to explain even what seemed very simple: "Down with the ten capitalist ministers!" The Mensheviks do not agree? Then "down with the Mensheviks!" They laugh? Let them: they will not laugh long; we shall see who will be the last to laugh.

I had put forward a proposal that the Congress should discuss urgently the problem of the new military offensive which was being prepared at the front. Lenin, I remember, approved of my suggestion, but he wanted to discuss it first with the other members of the Central Committee. Comrade Kamenev brought to the session Lenin's hastily sketched Bolshevik resolution concerning the offensive. I do not know whether this document still exists. The text, however, proved for one reason or another unacceptable either to the Bolsheviks or to the internationalists. Posern, who was charged with presenting the resolution, also found it inadequate. I drafted a different text which was agreed on and finally presented to the Congress. Our intervention was, if I am not mistaken, directed by Sverdlov whom I met for the first time during this Congress. He was then presiding over the Bolshevik faction.

Sverdlov was so small and so frail that one would have thought he was ill; yet there was something in him which gave the impression of authority and quiet strength. He presided over the discussion without raising his voice, without interrupting the speakers; he worked evenly and smoothly like a well-oiled engine. The secret of his success lay not in his talent for conducting the debate, but in the fact that he was extremely well acquainted with those present in the hall and also that he knew exactly what he was trying to achieve. Before each conference he would meet every delegate individually, would question him and sometimes also brief him. Even before he opened the conference, he already had a more or less clear general idea of what turn the discussion would take. But even without the preliminary conversations he knew better than anybody else in what way this or that party worker would react to every particular problem. The number of our comrades with whose political personalities Sverdlov was well acquainted, was quite considerable, if one applies the standards of that time. He was a born organizer and planner. He saw every political problem first of all in the light of its intrinsic meaning for the party organization: he saw immediately how particular people and particular groups would react to it and how the alignments inside the organization would shape themselves and what consequently the relationship between the party and the masses outside the organization would be. Almost automatically he was translating algebraic formulae into arithmetical realities. He was able to check the worth of important political slogans against revolutionary actuality.

After the demonstration of June 10th was banned, when the temperature at the First Congress of the Soviets was rising rapidly and Tseretelli threatened to disarm the Petersburg workers, I went with comrade Kamenev to the editorial offices of *Pravda*. After a short exchange of view, I wrote, at Lenin's suggestion, a draft of an address of the Central Committee to the Executive Committee.

At the offices of *Pravda* Lenin commented in a few words on Tseretelli's last speech, that of June 11th: "But he really was a revolutionary once—doing so many years of hard labour! And now this complete renunciation of his past." There was nothing political in that remark, nothing polemical; it was a passing reflection on the sad fate of a former heroic revolutionary. There was a tinge of sorrow and resentment in Lenin's tone, although he spoke curtly and dryly, because nothing was more distasteful to him than a show of sentimentality or psychological ratiocination.

On July 4th or 5th I saw Lenin (and Zinoviev?) at the Tauride Palace, I think. The offensive was repelled. The anti-Bolshevik fury of the ruling group was at its height. "Now they will shoot us all," said Lenin, "for them it is the best moment." Basically, his plan was to beat the retreat and, if necessary, to descend into illegality. This was one of those sharp turns in Lenin's strategy which followed, as usual, upon a rapid assessment of circumstances. Later on, at the time of the Third Congress of the Comintern, Lenin once said: "In July we committed not a few silly blunders." What he meant was that military action had been premature and that our demonstration had taken much too aggressive a form, if one measured our forces against the vastness of the country. All the more remarkable was the sober restraint with which Lenin viewed, on July 4th or 5th, the chances not only of revolution but also of its adversaries, for whom, he concluded, had come the best moment to shoot us all. Fortunately, our enemies possessed neither such logical acuteness, nor such determination. They were satisfied with chemical concoctions *à la* Perevertzev.[5] However, it was quite probable that if they had succeeded, immediately after the July demonstration, in laying their hands on Lenin, they, or rather their officers, would have done with him what less than two years later German *soldateska* did with Liebknecht and Rosa Luxemburg.

During our meeting mentioned above no clear decision to hide or to return to clandestinity was taken. The Kornilov revolt was only gradually taking shape. I myself remained 'in evidence' for another two or three days. At a few meetings of the party and of the organization I spoke on the subject: "What is to be done?" Wild attacks on the

Bolsheviks seemed irresistible. The Mensheviks tried by all means to take advantage of the situation which had arisen not without their assistance. I remember I had to speak in the Library of the Tauride Palace at a meeting of some representatives of professional trade unions. The top leaders only—in all a few dozen people—were present. The Mensheviks predominated. I kept on stressing how necessary it was for the professional trade unions to protest against the accusation of alleged Bolshevik links with German militarism. I now remember vaguely the course of this meeting, but I have still before me very clearly two or three spiteful faces as if begging to be slapped. . .

In the meantime terror was growing and arrests multiplied. I spent a few days hiding in the flat of Comrade Larin. Then I started going out; I put an appearance at the Tauride Palace and soon I was arrested. I was released only during the 'Kornilov days' when the Bolshevik wave was mounting. By that time the Inter-Borough Organization had already joined the Bolshevik Party. Sverdlov proposed that I should meet Lenin who was still in hiding. I do not remember who took me (was it Rakhia?) to a worker's lodging which had become Lenin's hiding place. There I also met Kalinin, whom Lenin continued, in my presence, to subject to thorough questioning: what was the mood of the workers? Would they fight? Would they fight to the end? Could we seize power? And so on, and so on.

What was Lenin's state of mind at that time? If I were to describe it in a few words I would say that it was one of controlled impatience and deep anxiety. He saw clearly that the moment was approaching when all would be at stake; at the same time he thought, not unreasonably, that the leadership of the party did not draw from this all the necessary conclusions. The attitude of the Central Committee was, according to him, too passive; they were waiting for something to turn up. He considered that it was impossible for him to return to work in the open; he rightly feared that if he were arrested, the wait-and-see attitude of the top leadership would become strengthened and even more fixed; this would unavoidably have led us to miss the exceptional revolutionary situation. Hence Lenin's extreme vigilance. During these days and weeks his denunciations of any sign of opportunism or procrastination and irresolution grew sharper and more violent than ever.

He demanded that a conspiracy should be organized immediately: the enemy caught unawares; power seized; and then, we shall see. . . However, all this I shall have to describe in more detail.

The biographer will have to consider with the greatest attention the question of Lenin's return to Russia and the way in which he came into contact with the Russian masses. Apart from a short period, in 1905, Lenin had spent 15 years as an émigré abroad. His sense of the real, his intimate understanding of the living and toiling worker had not weakened during these years at all; on the contrary, through theoretical study and his creative imagination it had become even more solid. From episodic and accidental encounters, from observation whenever an opportunity occurred, Lenin gathered details which allowed him to build up a whole.

However, it was as an émigré that he spent those years of his life during which he finally acquired the stature to play his future historical role. When he arrived in Petersburg, he brought with him those revolutionary conclusions which summed up all his social-theoretical work and all the practical experience of his life. He proclaimed the watchword of socialist revolution the minute he touched the soil of Russia. But only then, face to face with the awakening working masses of Russia, all the accumulated knowledge, all that had been pondered, and all that had been resolved, went on practical trial. The formulae stood the test. Moreover, only here in Russia, in Petersburg, in daily life, they took on a concrete irrefutable shape and consequently an irresistible force. Now there was no longer any need to construe the image of the whole from fragments gathered more or less accidentally. The entire reality asserted itself with the full voice of the revolution. And here Lenin demonstrated—or perhaps he himself realized it fully for the first time—to what degree his ear was attuned to the still discordant clamour of the awakening masses. With what profound, almost organic, contempt he viewed the mice-like scurrying of the leading parties of the February revolution, and the waves of 'powerful' public opinion beating upon one newspaper and another; with what scorn he looked at the shortsighted, self-satisfied, babbling official Russia of the February days! Behind this stage hung with democratic props, he heard the rumble of events on quite a different scale. When the sceptics were pointing to all the difficulties of his enterprise, to the mobilization of bourgeois public opinion, to the simplicity of the petty-bourgeoisie—he set his teeth, his muscles tense on his high cheek-bones. This meant that he was restraining himself from telling the sceptics plainly and bluntly what he thought of them. He saw and he understood the difficulties just as well as did the others; but he also had the almost physical awareness—as if it were tangible— of the gigantic historical forces pent up and now ready for the tremendous burst which was to overcome all obstacles. He saw, heard, and understood in the first instance, the Russian workers whose numbers grew, who had not forgotten the events of 1905, who had gone through the school of war with all its illusions, through the falsehood and lies of the 'defence of the nation', and were now prepared for the greatest sacrifices and unprecedented effort. He understood the soldier who, stunned by three years of senseless and absurd carnage, was now stirred by the thunder of revolution and was preparing to pay for all the needless sufferings, all the humiliations and blows with an outburst of hatred, sparing nobody.

He guessed the mood of the peasant, who still trailing behind him the chains of centuries of serfdom, now in the turmoil of war, saw for the first time the chance of settling scores with the oppressors, the exploiters, the landlords, and the masters. The *muzhik* was still helplessly shuffling along, wavering between the empty verbiage of Chernov and the old 'method' or agrarian revolt. The soldier was still dragging his feet looking for a way out between patriotism and foolish desertion. The workers were still half-listening, but with distrust and some hostility, to the last tirades of Tseretelli. The steam in the boilers of the Kronstadt warships was already hissing impatiently.

The sailor who had within himself all the hatreds of the worker, as sharp as a steel blade, and all the heavy bear-like wrath of the *muzhik*, this sailor, singed by the flames of the terrible war, was already throwing overboard all that in his eyes embodied tyranny: the whole social hierarchy and military and bureaucratic oppressors. The February revolution was on the way out. The rags of legality of the Tsarist regime were being picked up by a coalition of its saviours, stretching, mending, and patching them into a thin cloak of democratic legitimacy. But underneath everything was bubbling and boiling, and the old anger was coming to the top: there was the hatred of the bailiff and of the landlord, of the district officer, of the inspector, of the chief of the police, of the manager, of the usurer, of the factory owner, of the parasite, of the 'man with white hands', of the despot and the tyrant—this was the prelude to the greatest revolutionary upheaval. And this was what Lenin heard and what he saw. Immediately after his return to a country which was in the throes of revolution, he sensed all this with his whole being, with an extraordinary acuteness, with an absolute certainty.

"You imbeciles, braggarts, idiots, you think that history is made in drawing-rooms where upstart democrats fraternize with titled liberals, where miserable provincial pettifoggers of yesterday learn to kiss the gracious hands of their Eminences! Imbeciles, braggarts, idiots! History is made in the trenches where the soldier, possessed by the nightmare of war-madness, plunges his bayonet into the officer's stomach and then, clinging like grim death to the buffers of a train carriage, escapes to his native village there to set on fire his landlord's manor. You don't like this brutality? 'Don't get cross', answers history: you are treated to all that I possess. What happens now is simply the result of what went on before. Do you truly imagine that history is made in your 'contact commissions'? Nonsense, childish prattle, tomfoolery, stupidity. History—as all will soon see—this time has chosen as its workshop-laboratory the palace of Kshesinskaya, the ballerina, the one time mistress of the former Tsar. Here, in this edifice, so symbolic of the old Russia, history prepares the liquidation of our monarchical, bureaucratic, courtly, landed, and bourgeois corruption and squalor. To this palace of the former imperial ballerina flock sweaty factory delegates, grey, haggard, and lousy foot-envoys from the trenches and from here they carry throughout the country their prophetic message."

Woeful ministers of the revolution deliberated and meditated how to give back the palace to its rightful owner. The newspapers of the Social Revolutionaries, of the Mensheviks, of the bourgeois parties were gnashing their rotten teeth, because from the balcony of the Kshesinskaya Palace Lenin's call for social upheaval was resounding. But their belated efforts could neither increase Lenin's hatred of the old Russia, nor strengthen his will to settle accounts with her. Both his hatred and his will reached their final limit. On the Kshesinskaya balcony stood Lenin, the same man who two months later would be hiding in a hayloft; and, after that, in a few weeks at most, would become the Chairman of the People's Commissars.

At the same time Lenin saw that within the party itself there was a conservative opposition (at first not so much political as psychological) to the great leap which had now to be made. Lenin watched with anxiety the growing divergence between the mood of some leaders and that of the working masses. His apprehension was not allayed by the fact that the Central Committee adopted the formula of armed rising. He knew all the difficulties of passing from words to deeds. Persistently and by all means available to him, he strove to subject the party to the pressure of the masses and the Central Committee to the pressure of the rank and file of the party. At the same time, he was acutely aware that there was no time to be lost. It is impossible to maintain a revolutionary situation at will until such moment as the party is ready to make use of it. This we have learned recently from the German experience. Even not so long ago some people argued: if we had not seized power in October, we would have seized it two or three months later. This is a profoundly mistaken view. Had we not seized power in October, we would not have seized it at all. Before October our strength lay precisely in the fact that the masses were pouring into our party because they believed that *it* would do what others had failed to do. If the working classes had detected in us the slightest sign of vacillation, of *'attentisme'*, or of a divergence between our words and our deeds, within two or three months the tide would have ebbed away just as it ebbed away from the SRs and the Mensheviks. The bourgeoisie would have obtained a respite and would have used it for concluding the peace. The whole relation of forces would have been radically changed and the proletarian upheaval would have been postponed indefinitely. Lenin understood and sensed and felt this; hence his anxiety and fear, his distrust and his frantic pressure which saved the revolution.

The dissensions within the party which came violently to the surface during the days of October had already made their appearance previously at various stages of the revolution. The first conflict over principles was still conducted in the calm manner in which theoretical questions are debated. It arose immediately after Lenin's return to Russia in connection with his 'April theses'. A little later the dull thud of the second clash could be heard: here was the question of the demonstration of armed workers on April 20th. The third disagreement arose over armed demonstration of June 10th: 'the moderates' maintained that Lenin schemed to implicate them in a demonstration which would have led to an armed rising. The next conflict, a much sharper one, occurred as a result of the July Days. This time the disagreements were reported by the newspapers. The problem of the Pre-parliament became another subject of inner party struggle, in which two openly contesting groups stood face to face. Were any minutes made during the party session? Has any report of it been preserved? The discussions were undoubtedly of tremendous interest. Two distinct factions made their appearance: one demanding the seizure of power; the other determined to enter the Constituent Assembly and there to play the role of opposition. Those who were against participation in the Pre-parliament were in a minority, though the majority of the other group was not very considerable. To the debates and to the final decision Lenin reacted immediately. From his hiding-place he wrote to the Central Committee, expressing with great vigour his solidarity with those who refused to enter the Bulygin Duma—the Pre-parliament of Kerensky and Tseretelli. I do not find this letter in the second part of volume XIV of Lenin's *Works*. Has this extremely valuable document been preserved?[6]

The dissensions reached their climax immediately before October when, finally, the party was to enter the road of revolution and fix the date of the uprising. Later, after October 25th (November 7th in the new calendar), the tension became even sharper when the problem of the coalition with other socialist parties was debated.

It would be highly interesting to reconstruct in all its concrete details Lenin's role on the eve of April 20th, of June 10th, and just before the July Days. "In July we committed a lot of blunders," Lenin used to say later, not only in private conversations but also at meetings with the German delegates after the March rising of 1921 in Germany. What were these "blunders"? Energetic, perhaps too energetic experiments; trying to find out hastily, perhaps too

---

[6] The letter has been published in vol. XXXIV, p. 342, edition 5 of Lenin's *Sochinenya*, Moscow, 1962. (Translator's note.)

hastily, how far we could press forward. From time to time this kind of reconnoitring was necessary, otherwise we would have lost contact with the masses. On the other hand, it is well known that scouts too rash in advance may sometimes—whether one wants it or not—involve one in a major battle. This did not happen in July. The retreat was sounded in time. Furthermore, the enemy lacked courage to go the whole hog. This was no matter of chance; the Kerensky regime in its very essence was a regime of half-measures; this craven Kerenskism all the more successfully paralysed the adventurer Kornilov, the more afraid of him it was itself.

3
The Uprising

THE DATE of the Second Congress of the Soviets was set, at our insistence, to coincide with the end of the Democratic Conference, that is for October 25th. In view of the fever of agitation which was mounting from hour to hour, not only in the workers' districts but also in the soldiers' barracks, it seemed to us that it would be most expedient to focus the attention of the Petersburg garrison on that particular day on which the Congress of the Soviets would have to decide the question of the seizure of power. The workers and the soldiers, being properly prepared for this, would proclaim their support for the Congress. Our strategy was, in fact, an offensive one: we advanced to win power; but our propaganda was based on the assumption that enemies were intent on dispersing the Congress of the Soviets and that therefore we had to repulse them ruthlessly. In this whole plan we relied on the powerful tide of revolution which was rising all the time everywhere and was allowing the enemy no respite and no repose. Even the most backward regiments remained, at worst, neutral. In such conditions the government's slightest move against the Petrograd Soviet would have immediately assured our decisive preponderance. Lenin, however, feared that the adversary might succeed in bringing in a small but resolutely counter-revolutionary number of troops, might attack first and in this way gain the advantage of surprise. By catching the party and the Soviet off their guard, by arresting the top leaders in Petrograd, the enemy would in this way decapitate the whole movement and then, gradually, render it powerless. "We dare not wait, we dare not delay," urged Lenin.

Such was the situation when, at the end of September or at the beginning of October the now famous night session of the Central Committee took place in the Sukhanovs' flat. Lenin arrived absolutely determined this time to carry through such a resolution as would leave no room for doubt, vacillation, procrastination, passivity, and delay.

Moreover, even before he had taken his stand against the opponents of the armed rising, he rebuked those who connected the uprising with the Second Congress of the Soviets. Somebody told him that I had said "We have already fixed the date of the rising for 25 October." I had indeed repeatedly said this, when I argued against those comrades who saw the road of revolution leading through pre-parliament and through 'impressive' Bolshevik opposition in the Constituent Assembly. "If the Congress of the Soviets, where the Bolsheviks are in a majority, will not take power," I maintained, "then Bolshevism, as a whole, will have to pay a heavy price for this. In that case the Constituent Assembly will probably not be convened at all. By the mere fact that after all that had happened before, we did convene for October 25th the Congress of the Soviets which, we knew beforehand, had an assured Bolshevik majority, we have publicly pledged ourselves to seize power not later than on that date."

Vladimir Ilyich protested violently. The question of the Second Congress of the Soviets, he said, was of no interest to him: what importance had it at all? Would the Congress take place? And suppose that it did take place, what would follow? We had to win power and not to tie ourselves to the Congress. It was ridiculous and absurd to warn the enemy about the date of the rising. At best, the date of October 25th could be used to hoodwink the enemy, but it was imperative that the rising should break out sooner and independently of the Congress. First the party must seize power, arms in hand, and then we could talk about the Congress. We should pass over to action immediately.

As in the July Days, when Lenin definitely expected that 'they' would shoot us all, he now analysed the whole situation from the point of view of our enemies: the bourgeoisie would gain most if it attacked us suddenly, disrupting the revolution and then finishing it off bit by bit. As in July, so now, Lenin overrated both the shrewdness and the vigour—and perhaps the material possibilities too—of our opponents. To some degree Lenin's appraisal of the enemy had a purpose which was tactically correct: by over-estimating the enemy's forces he aimed at stimulating the party and provoking it to redouble its efforts.

And yet the party could not seize power by itself, independently of the Soviets and behind its back. This would have been a mistake, the consequences of which would have affected the attitude of the workers and might have had harmful repercussions within the Petersburg garrison. The soldiers knew their delegates in the Soviet; it was through the Soviet that they knew the party. If the uprising had taken place behind the back of the Soviet, independently of it, without its authority and not openly and for all to see as a further step in the struggle for power, there might have been a dangerous confusion among the troops. Besides, one should not forget that in Petersburg, side by side with the local Soviet, there still existed the old All-Russian Central Executive Committee at the head of which stood the SRs and the Mensheviks. Only the Congress of the Soviets could be set against this Committee.

After all, in the Central Committee itself there existed three distinct factions: first, those who opposed the seizure of power and whose logic of the situation led them to reject the slogan 'all power to the Soviets'; second, Lenin, who demanded the immediate organization of the uprising, independently of the Soviets; and the third faction, which considered it imperative to link the uprising closely with the Second Congress of the Soviets so that even the date of the two events should coincide. "In any case", insisted Lenin, "the rising must precede the Congress, otherwise they will disperse you and you will have no chance to convene the Congress." Finally, according to the proposed resolution, the uprising was to take place not later than October 15th. About this, as far as I remember, there was hardly any discussion. Everybody understood that this was an approximate date, a point of time, as it were, which could, according to circumstances, be advanced or delayed, but only for a matter of days. The need for a 'deadline' and a close one at that, was absolutely clear.

The main debates at the sessions of the Central Committee were, of course, devoted to the struggle against the fraction which opposed armed rising altogether. I would not undertake to reproduce here Lenin's three or four interventions during the last session, when he discussed the following questions: Should we seize power? Is it time to seize power? Will we be able to remain in power after the insurrection? At that period and also later Lenin wrote many pamphlets and articles dealing with these problems. His way of reasoning, when he addressed the session, was, of course, the same; it is impossible, however, to convey the general atmosphere, the tenseness of these passionate improvisations permeated through and through with the effort to impart to critics, to the hesitant, to the doubting his own thought, his own willpower, his own conviction and his courage. The destiny of revolution was in the balance. The meeting ended late at night. Every one of us felt like a patient after a surgical operation. Together with a few comrades I spent the rest of that night in Sukhanov's home.

The further course of events, as is well known, helped us a great deal. The attempt to disband the local garrison resulted in the formation of a revolutionary war committee. Now we were in a position to 'legalize' our preliminaries for the uprising, to back them by the authority of the Soviet, and also to show how vital our cause was for all the troops in Petrograd. In the short spell of time between the session of the Central Committee in Sukhanov's home and October 25th I met Vladimir Ilyich only once, I think, and even this one meeting I recall rather hazily. When was it? It must have been some time between October 15th and 25th. I remember that I was very curious to learn what Lenin's reaction had been to the 'defensive' character of the speech I made at the session of the Petrograd Soviet: I had branded as false all the rumours according to which we were preparing an armed rising for October 22nd (which was 'The Day of the Proletarian Soviet'); at the same time I had warned that we would meet every attack against us with a merciless and resolute counter-attack. When I saw Vladimir Ilyich it struck me that he was in a rather serene and confident mood, and, I should say, he was less suspicious. He not only had nothing critical to say about my speech, he even approved of it, considering its defensive tone useful as a means to lull the vigilance of the enemy. He, nevertheless, kept on shaking his head and asking: "Won't they forestall us? Won't they attack all of a sudden?" I was trying to prove that from now on everything would go on almost automatically. During that conversation, or at least during a part of it, Comrade Stalin was present, if I am not mistaken. It might be, however, that I am here compressing two meetings into one. Generally speaking, I must admit that my recollections of the last few days before the actual upheaval became extremely confused and as if telescoped in my memory, so that it is difficult for me to sort them out and establish clearly the time and place of every incident.

My next meeting with Lenin occurred on the very day of October 25th, in the Smolny Institute. At what time? I have no idea, but it must have been towards evening. I well remember the anxious tone of his first inquiry about the state of negotiations which we were conducting with the General Staff of the Petrograd district concerning the future of the local garrison. The newspapers had just announced that the negotiations were nearing a favourable conclusion. "So you are aiming at a compromise solution, are you?" asked Lenin, his glance piercing us. I answered that we had 'leaked' to the newspapers this reassuring piece of news on purpose: this was our *ruse de guerre* just before the general battle. "Ah, that's good, good, excellent," he sang out joyfully and gaily; he started pacing up and down the room vigorously, rubbing his hands energetically: "That's ve-ry excellent!" Military stratagems always appealed to him. To deceive the enemy, to make him look foolish—wasn't this a delightful prospect! In this case the cunning manoeuvre had quite a special significance: it really meant that we had embarked directly upon the decisive course of action. I related to him that our military operations were already well advanced and that several important points of the city were in our hands. Vladimir Ilyich noticed (or perhaps I showed him) a poster printed the day before in which we threatened with summary execution any person caught in the act of plunder or looting during the uprising. At first Lenin seemed disconcerted, even a little doubtful perhaps. But then he said: "Well, that's right." With breathless impatience he kept on inquiring about the smallest details: for him they constituted irrefutable proof that this time the tide of events was irreversible, that the Rubicon had been crossed, that there was no possibility of retreat, no way back. He was, I remember, greatly impressed by the fact that in a written order I called upon the Pavlovsky regiment to secure the safety of the presses in which party and Soviet newspapers were being printed.

"And what, the regiment came out?"

"Yes, it did."

"And the papers are going to be published?"

"Yes, they are."

Lenin was overjoyed; he was cheerful, laughing, rubbing his hands. Then he lapsed into silence, thought for a while, and said:

"Oh, all right, one can proceed in this fashion as well, provided we seize power."

I understood that it was only then that he finally made peace with the fact that we were not proceeding by way of a conspiracy and a plot. But till the very end he was apprehensive lest the enemy thwarted our plans, or attacked us, throwing us off balance. Only now, that is on the evening of October 25th, he became more composed and gave his definite approval to the manner in which affairs were being conducted. I said that he became "more composed", but then he immediately started worrying about a whole series of problems, small and not so small, material, and less so, connected with the further course of events.

"Listen," he would say, "wouldn't it be better to do this in such a way? Shouldn't we try and do this or that? Wouldn't it be advisable to appeal to so and so? Or call out such and such?"

All these interminable questions and suggestions may have seemed disconnected, but they all had the same source: the intensity of the thought which with one great sweep embraced the totality of the revolution.

One has to learn not to lose one's breath in the rush of revolutionary events. When the tide is flowing strongly, when the forces of the revolution are automatically gathering strength, and the forces of reaction are scattering and fritter away, then there is the great temptation to let oneself be carried by the elemental power of the mighty wave. Success too quick may be as dangerous as defeat. Not to lose sight of the guiding line of events; after each new success to tell oneself: nothing has been achieved yet, nothing made quite secure; five minutes before final victory to act with the same vigilance, the same energy and the same tenacity with which one acted five minutes before the beginning of the military operations; five minutes after victory, even before the first triumphant applause has sounded, to remind oneself: What has been conquered has not yet been secured and no time must be lost—such was the attitude, such was the manner and such was the method of Lenin; such was the organic essence of his political character and revolutionary spirit.

*

I have already described elsewhere how Dan, going probably to one of the meetings of the Menshevik faction of the Second Congress of the Soviets, recognized Lenin in his disguise. We were sitting with Vladimir Ilyich at a small table in one of the rooms through which people had to pass. This scene has already become a subject of a painting which, however, as far as I can judge from the photographs, in no way conveys the reality of the situation. This, incidentally, applies to all historic paintings, and to other arts as well. I do not remember in what circumstances, much later, I said to Vladimir Ilyich:

"One should make a note of this incident, otherwise people will tell lies about it."

He waved his hand in a comic gesture of helplessness:

"It doesn't matter—there will be no end to lies anyhow . . ."

Lenin did not take part in the first session of the Second Congress of the Soviets in the big hall of the Smolny Institute. He remained in one of the adjoining rooms, in which, as I remember, there was for some reason very little furniture, or perhaps none at all. Later somebody spread two sheets on the floor and placed two cushions on them. We were both resting, lying down side by side. But after a few minutes I was called:

"Dan is speaking—you have to answer."

After having given my rebuttal to Dan, I went back to lie down again. Vladimir Ilyich did not even think of falling asleep. How could one? Every five or ten minutes somebody would run in from the hall to tell us what was going on there. Apart from this, messengers were arriving from the city where the troops, commanded by Antonov-Ovseenko, were laying siege to the Winter Palace; our assault had to end the siege.

Next morning I think it was, the morning which only a sleepless night separated from the previous day, I glanced at the tired face of Vladimir Ilyich. Smiling, he said:

"Too sudden a transition from clandestinity and the

regime of Perevertzev—to power . . . *Es schwindelt.* (One gets dizzy.)'

I do not know why he said it in German. He supplemented his words with an eloquent gesture of his hand: round and round his forehead. After this single more or less personal remark, which I heard from him in connection with the seizure of power, we passed on to deal with current affairs.

4
Brest-Litovsk

TO AROUSE the masses of Germany, of Austro-Hungary, as well as of the Entente—this was what we hoped to achieve by entering into peace negotiations. Having this aim in mind, we reasoned that the negotiations should drag on as long as possible, in this way giving the European workers enough time to acquire a proper understanding of the actuality of the revolution, and more especially, of the revolution's policy of peace. After the first breakdown of peace talks, Lenin proposed that I should go to Brest-Litovsk. By itself the prospect of talks with Baron Kühlmann and General Hoffmann was hardly attractive, but, as Lenin expressed himself, "in order to temporize a temporizer is needed." At the Smolny we had briefly exchanged ideas as to the general line of negotiations. The question whether we should sign the peace or not was for the time being postponed: it was impossible to foresee what course the negotiations would take, what effect they would produce in Europe, and what the general situation would be. We had not, of course, given up hope of some revolutionary developments.

That we were not in a position to go on fighting was absolutely evident to me. On my way to Brest-Litovsk, passing through the front line, I realized that our comrades, regardless of all warnings and exhortations, were quite unable to organize any kind of demonstration against Germany's excessive demands: the trenches were almost empty; nobody dared to utter a word about the continuation of war under any conditions. "Peace, peace, whatever happens!"

Later, after my return from Brest-Litovsk, I tried to per-
suade a representative of the military faction of the All-
Russian Central Executive Committee that he should support
our delegation by making a 'patriotic' speech. "Impossible,"
he answered, "quite impossible; we would not be able to
return to the trenches—nobody would understand us; we
would lose all influence. . ." A revolutionary war was impossible—about this there was not the slightest shade of disagreement between Vladimir Ilyich and myself.

The question was: would the Germans be able to fight,
would they be able to launch an attack against a revolution
which proclaimed the end of hostilities? How could we find
this out, how could we probe the mood of the German
masses and of the German soldiers? What impression had
the February and then the October revolution made on
them? The January strikes in Germany indicated that some
upheaval had started. How serious was it? Should one not
put the German working classes and the German army to
the test: On the one hand, proletarian revolution proclaiming the end of the war; on the other, the Hohenzollern
regime ordering the launching of an offensive against that
very revolution.

"Certainly, this is very tempting," objected Lenin, "and
no doubt such a test will have its impact. But it's risky, very
risky. And German militarism may prove sufficiently powerful to launch an offensive against us—what then? No, we
cannot take the risk: at the moment there is nothing more
important in the world than our revolution."

The dispersal of the Constituent Assembly at first made
our international situation much worse. The Germans had
still feared that we might come to an understanding with
the 'patriotic' Constituent Assembly and that this might
result in an attempt to continue the war. Such an attempt
would have been senseless and would have led to a final
defeat both of the revolution and of the country. But this
would have become obvious only later on; in the meantime
the Germans would have had to make one more effort. Did

they see the dispersal of the Constituent Assembly as evidence of our readiness to put an end to hostilities at no matter what price?

Kühlmann became immediately more insolent. What could have been the reaction of the working class of the Entente to the dispersal of the Assembly? To this question it was easy to find an answer: The Press of the Entente treated the Soviet regime simply as an agency of the Hohenzollerns—there you are: the Bolsheviks disperse the 'democratic' Assembly in order to conclude with the Germans an infamous peace just at the time when Belgium and northern France are under German occupation. It was quite clear that the bourgeois press of the West would succeed in spreading terrible confusion among the working classes. This, in turn, would facilitate military intervention against us. It was well-known that, even in Germany, in the circles of the social-democratic opposition, there were persistent rumours alleging that the Bolsheviks were in the pay of the German government and that what went on at Brest-Litovsk was only a comedy in which the roles had been assigned to the actors in advance. How much more credible such a version of events must have seemed to the French and to the English!

I maintained that before we proceeded to sign the peace it was absolutely imperative that we should prove to the workers of Europe, in a most striking manner, how great, how deadly, was our hatred for the rulers of Germany. Precisely these considerations led me, during my stay in Brest-Litovsk, to have recourse to an 'instructive' presentation of our attitude which was summed up in the formula: we stop the war but do not sign the peace. I consulted the other members of the delegation who gave their assent and I wrote to Vladimir Ilyich. He answered: we shall discuss this when you come back. It is possible that by this kind of answer Lenin actually hinted at his disagreement. I do not remember this clearly at the present moment of time and I have not his letter at hand—I am not even sure it has been preserved. After my return we had long discussions with Vladimir Ilyich in the Smolny.

"All this is very attractive and one could wish for nothing better, if only General Hoffmann were not strong enough to throw his troops against us. But of this there is little hope. For his purposes he will find hand-picked regiments of rich Bavarian peasants—he does not need many. . . You yourself say that our trenches are deserted. And what if he really renews hostilities?"

"Then we shall be forced to sign the peace, but it will become clear to all that we have no other way out. This by itself will decisively dispose of the legends that we have some behind-the-scenes links with the Hohenzollern."

"To be sure, there are advantages. . . And yet there are too many risks. At the moment there is nothing more important in the world than our revolution; the revolution has to be safeguarded no matter what the price."

To the essential difficulties of the situation were added considerable complications within the party. In the party, or at least among its leading personalities, the dominant mood was one of intransigence: we should reject German conditions and refuse to sign the peace. The reports which our newspapers published about the course of negotiations maintained and sharpened this mood, which found its most striking expression among the left communists who put forward the slogan of revolutionary war. Lenin, of course, became alarmed by such developments.

"If the Central Committee decides to accept the German conditions, presented in the form of a verbal ultimatum only, we are running the risk of a split in the party," I argued. "Our party, no less than the workers of Europe, must be made clearly aware of the real state of affairs. . . If we break with the left wing, the party will make a sharp turn to the right: it is a fact that those comrades who were militantly against the October insurrection and for the alliance with socialist parties, are now unreservedly for peace. And the signing of peace is not our only task. Among the left communists are some of the most active fighters for the revolution. . ."

"All this is undeniable," answered Vladimir Ilyich, "but the fate of the revolution is at stake. We shall re-establish a balance in the party, but first of all we must save the revolution, and we can save the revolution only by signing the peace. Better a split in the party than the danger of a military defeat of the revolution. The leftists will cease making trouble, and then—even if they provoke the split, which is by no means certain—they will come back to the party. If the Germans crush us, then there will be nobody to come back. . . All right, suppose that we accept your plan. We have refused to sign the peace, and then the Germans launch an offensive. What do you do then?"

"We sign the peace at the points of their bayonets. The moral of the scene is obvious to the working class of the whole world."

"And then will you not support the slogan of a revolutionary war?"

"Under no circumstances."

"If this is so, then the experiment may not be so very dangerous. We may lose Esthonia and Latvia. Esthonian comrades came to see me and described to me how well they have succeeded in introducing the socialist system in the countryside. It would be a great pity to sacrifice a socialist Esthonia", added Lenin with a smile, "but we may have to, we may have to do this for the sake of peace."

"And if the peace is signed immediately—does this exclude the possibility of German military intervention in Esthonia or Latvia?"

"All right, may be not. But there it is a possibility, while here we face a certainty. I, in any case, I shall declare myself for immediate peace. This seems more sure."

The main danger which Lenin saw in my plan consisted in this: in the event of a new German offensive, we would not manage to sign the peace, because German militarism would leave us no time to do so. "German militarism is a beast that moves swiftly," Vladimir Ilyich kept on repeating. At meetings at which the question of peace was debated, Lenin spoke sharply against the left, and with calm and circumspection against my plan. However, later he accepted it though very reluctantly: the party was obviously opposed to the signing of peace and it was felt that a kind of intermediate decision might constitute a bridge leading towards some compromise solution.

A conference of the most prominent Bolsheviks, that is of the delegates to the Third Congress of the Soviets, showed beyond all doubt that our party, having so recently emerged from the hot furnace of October, had to test in action the international situation for itself. If there were no intermediate formula, the majority would have pronounced itself for the revolutionary war.

It is perhaps worth noting that the left Social Revolutionaries were not straightway against the Brest-Litovsk peace. In any case, Spiridonova was at first decidedly for signing. "The muzhik does not want war," she said, "and he will accept any kind of peace."

"Sign the treaty at once," she told me when I first returned from Brest, "and abolish the grain monopoly." Later on, the left SRs supported the intermediate formula of ending the hostilities without signing any peace; but they considered the formula as a step towards proclaiming the revolutionary war—"in case of need."

We knew that the German representatives received our declaration in a way which suggested that Germany had no intention of renewing the offensive. Such was the conclusion with which we returned to Moscow.

"Won't they cheat us?" Lenin was asking. With an expansive gesture of our hands we meant to indicate that it was rather unlikely.

"Oh, well," said Lenin, "if so that's all to the good. *Les apparences*[1] (appearances) are saved and here we are,

---

[1] In French in the original text.

out of the war." (The conversations in this chapter are not, of course, quoted word for word, but the expression "*les apparences*" I remember literally.)

However, two days before the expiry of the truce, we received from our General Samoylo, who had remained at Brest, a telegram informing us that according to General Hoffmann's communication, Germany considered itself from midday, February 18th, to be in a state of war with us and therefore requested Samoylo to leave Brest-Litovsk. The first to receive this telegram was Vladimir Ilyich. I was in his office. We had been talking with Karelin and with some other comrade belonging to the left Social Revolutionaries.

Having glanced at the text, Lenin handed it to me without a word. From his expression I immediately guessed that here was an important and grave piece of news. Lenin hastened to end the conversation with the Social Revolutionaries—he wanted to discuss the sudden turn of events.

"In spite of everything they cheated us. They gained five days. . . This beast will not let go a thing. That means that now there is nothing left but to sign the old conditions, if only the Germans will still stick to them."

I argued that we should let Hoffmann actually go over to the offensive.

"But that means that we shall have to give up Dvinsk, lose a great deal of artillery, and so on?"

"Yes, of course, this means fresh sacrifices. But I think that the German soldier should in fact step on to the Soviet territory arms in hand. And this should be made known to the German workers on the one side, and to the French and English workers on the other."

"No," contradicted Lenin. "Of course, it is not a matter of Dvinsk. Now not an hour must be wasted. We have made the experiment. Hoffmann wants to fight and is able to fight. It is impossible to delay: they have already robbed us of five days which I wanted to make use of. This beast leaps fast."

The Central Committee took the decision to send a telegram expressing our readiness to sign the peace treaty immediately. The telegram was duly dispatched.

"It seems to me," I said to Lenin in a private conversation, "that politically it would be expedient if I resigned as a Commissar for Foreign Affairs."

"What for? We do not want to introduce these parliamentary procedures here."

"But my resignation would be seen by the Germans as a radical shift in policy; it would strengthen their trust that this time we are really prepared to sign the peace and abide by it."

"That's possible," answered Lenin thoughtfully. "This is a weighty political argument."

I do not remember at what precise moment we received the news about the German invasion of Finland and about the attack on the Finnish workers. I recall that I came across Vladimir Ilyich in the corridor, near his office. He was extremely agitated. I have never seen him in such a state, never before nor after.

"Well, well," he said, "it looks as if we have to fight, though we have nothing to fight with. This time, it seems, there is no other way out..."

Such was Lenin's first reaction to the news of the defeat of the Finnish revolution. But already ten or fifteen minutes later, when I entered his office, he said:

"No, we should not change our policy. Our action would not have saved revolutionary Finland, but without any doubt would have brought our ruin. We shall do whatever we can to help the Finnish workers—but short of war and still maintaining peace. I do not know whether this will still save us now. In any case, this is our only road to salvation."

And indeed salvation came that way.

The refusal to sign the peace treaty was not, as it is now maintained, the result of an abstract idea that any agreement between us and the imperialists was unthinkable. It is enough to consult a pamphlet by Comrade Ovsyannikov, in which he described an extremely illuminating survey conducted by Lenin on this subject. The survey proves convincingly that the partisans of the tentative policy of 'neither war nor peace' answered 'Yes' to the question whether we, as a revolutionary party, were entitled to sign, in a certain situation, a 'shameful' peace. As a matter of fact, we did maintain that if there were only twenty-five chances in a hundred that the Hohenzollern would decide not to fight, or if he found that he was in no position to fight, we would have to take the risk and make the experiment.

Three years later we took another chance—this one at Lenin's initiative—to sound, with the help of our bayonets, the situation in Poland, the Poland of the bourgeoisie and petty nobility. We were repulsed. What was then the difference between the Polish 'sounding' and the Brest-Litovsk test? As to the general principle, there was no difference; there was only one in the degree of the risk we took.

Comrade Radek once wrote, I remember, that the powerful sweep of Lenin's tactical ideas could best be noticed in the period between the signature of the Brest-Litovsk treaty and the march on Warsaw. Now we all know that the march on Warsaw was a very costly mistake, resulting not only in the conclusion of the Riga Treaty which cut us off from Germany, but also, together with other contemporary developments, it helped tremendously in the consolidation of bourgeois Europe. The counter-revolutionary character of the Riga Treaty and its influence on the fate of Europe becomes quite obvious if one imagines the course events might have taken during one year only, during 1923, if we had had a common frontier with Germany: there are innumerable reasons to think that the German developments would have shaped themselves in an entirely different manner. Nor can one doubt that without our military intervention—and our defeat—the revolutionary movement within

Poland would have taken on an incomparably more favourable aspect. As far as I am aware, Lenin himself attached a great importance to the 'Warsaw blunder'. And yet in his appraisal of Lenin's tactical *élan*, Radek was quite correct. Of course, after we failed to achieve the hoped-for results from our 'sounding' of the Polish working masses, after we were thrown back—and this was unavoidable because in the political calm which reigned in Poland our intervention could be nothing more than a guerrilla raid—and after we were compelled to sign the Riga Treaty, it was easy to come to the conclusion that the opponents of the march on Warsaw were right, that it would have been better to call a halt in time and render secure our frontier with Germany. Hindsight made all this clear. What was so striking in the whole enterprise was the audacity and courage of Lenin's conception. The risk was extraordinary; but so was the magnitude of the goal. The possible failure did not threaten the very existence of the Soviet state; at the most it might have weakened our country.

We can leave to the future historian the task of judging whether it was worth accepting worse conditions at Brest for the sake of exposing them to the full view of the European working masses. It was absolutely clear that once we had exposed them, we had no choice but to sign what was forced upon us. And here Lenin saved the situation by his clear and precise thinking and his resolution.

"And if the Germans maintain their offensive? And if they march on Moscow?"

"Then we shall withdraw farther east, to the Urals, all the time declaring our readiness to conclude peace. The Kuznets Basin is rich in coal. We shall set up an Uralo-Kuznets Republic based on the regional industry and the Kuznets coal and, supported by the proletariat of Ural and by as many workers as we shall manage to move with us from Moscow and Petrograd, we shall hold out. If need be, we shall retreat even deeper, beyond the Urals. We may reach Kamchatka, but we shall hold out. The international situation will be changing a dozen times; from the redoubt of our Uralo-Kuznets Republic, we shall spread out again and we shall return to Moscow and Petersburg. But now, if we senselessly involve ourselves in a revolutionary war, if we let the élite of our working class and our party perish, then, of course, we shall return nowhere."

At that time the Uralo-Kuznets Republic formed an important part of Lenin's arguments. His opponents were often disconcerted when he threw at them the question: "And do you realize that our coalfields in the Kuznets Basin are enormous? Together with the Ural iron ore and the Siberian grain we have a new base." Not always knowing where precisely the Kuznets Basin was situated nor what the possible relationship between its coal and Bolshevism and the revolutionary war was, Lenin's interlocutor would either gaze with wide open eyes or burst out laughing, not quite sure whether Lenin was joking or playing a trick on him. But, as a matter of fact, Lenin was by no means joking; true to himself, he was analysing the situation through to its very end, to its worst possibilities. To him the concept of the Uralo-Kuznets Republic was absolutely necessary in order to strengthen his own—and other people's—conviction that all was not lost and that there was no room, that there could be no room, for the strategy of despair.

Fortunately, we never were reduced to the Uralo-Kuznets Republic. Nevertheless one can assert that the Uralo-Kuznets Republic, which had never materialized, saved the Union of Russian Soviet Federal Socialist Republics.

In any case, to understand and appreciate Lenin's tactics during the Brest-Litovsk period, one has to view them together with his policy during October. To have taken a stand against the October uprising and for the Brest-Litovsk peace was, in fact, to express in both instances nothing else but the mood of capitulation. The essence of the matter is that Lenin approached the Brest-Litovsk capitulation with the same inexhaustible revolutionary energy which secured the party's victory in October. Precisely this intrinsic, and as if organic, combination of October and Brest-Litovsk, of the gigantic sweep with intrepidity and circumspection, of both boldness and foresight, gives a measure of Lenin's method and of his power.

5
The Dispersal of the Constituent Assembly

L ENIN raised the question of the Constituent Assembly
a few days, or even a few hours, after the insurrection.

"It has to be adjourned," he declared, "and the elections
have to be postponed. We must widen the electoral law so
that the eighteen-year-olds have the right to vote. We must
have time to revise the lists of candidates. Even our own
lists are not worth much: they contain a large number of
men from the intelligentsia, whose names appear almost
accidentally. What we need are workers and peasants. The
Kornilovists, the Cadets, should be outlawed."

Some protested: "It is awkward to postpone now. People
will see in this an attempt to liquidate the Assembly,
especially as we ourselves have accused the Provisional
Government of tampering with it."

"Nonsense!" objected Lenin. "Deeds are important, not
words. In relation to the Provisional Government the Constituent Assembly represented, or might have represented,
progress; in relation to the regime of the Soviets, and with
the existing electoral lists, it will inevitably mean retro-
gression. Why is it inconvenient to postpone it? Will it
be convenient if the Constituent Assembly turns out to
be composed of a Cadet-Menshevik-Social Revolutionary
alliance?"

"By that time we shall be stronger," remonstrated other
comrades, "we are still too weak now. The provinces hardly
know anything about the Soviet regime and if the news

spreads that we have adjourned the Assembly, we shall be weakened even further."

Sverdlov, who more than others was connected with the provinces, protested vehemently against the adjournment.

Lenin stood alone. He kept on shaking his head, dissatisfied, and went on repeating:

"You are wrong; it's clearly a mistake which can prove very costly. Let us hope that the revolution will not have to pay for it with its life. . ."

Yet when the decision not to postpone the elections was taken, Lenin devoted all his attention to organizational matters connected with the preliminaries to the Assembly. In the meantime it became evident that we would be in a minority, even if the left Social Revolutionaries gave us their support; the fact was that they had common lists with their right-wingers and were tricked all around.

"Of course, the Constituent Assembly should be dissolved," Lenin kept on saying, "but what to do with the left Social Revolutionaries?"

Old Natanson gave us a great deal of encouragement. He came to 'consult' us, and right from the beginning said:

"Well, I think that nevertheless the Assembly will have to be scattered by force."

"Bravo!" exclaimed Lenin, "That's right, that's right! But will your people agree to this?"

"Some are hesitant, but I believe that in the end they will agree," answered Natanson.

This was the heyday of the left Social Revolutionaries' extreme radicalism: they did indeed agree to the dispersal of the Constituent Assembly.

"And, suppose we unite our faction in the Constituent Assembly and your faction with the Central Executive Committee and in this way form a Convention?" proposed Natanson.

"What for?" asked Lenin, visibly annoyed. "To imitate the French Revolution? The dispersal of the Constituent Assembly will consolidate the Soviet system. Your plan will muddle everything up: we shall have neither fish nor flesh . . . "

Natanson tried to prove that by acting according to his plan we would be able to rub off some of the Assembly's authority onto our shoulders; but soon he was persuaded to give up his idea.

Lenin undertook to deal with the problem of the Assembly there and then.

"The mistake is obvious," he argued, "We have gained power and at the same time we have put ourselves into a position in which we are compelled to use military means in order to win it anew."

He was preparing the action against the Assembly extremely carefully, giving a great deal of thought to every detail and subjecting Uritsky, who, to his distress, had been appointed the Commissar for the Constituent Assembly, to intense interrogation. Among other measures, he also demanded that one of the Latvian regiments, consisting almost entirely of workers, be posted to Petrograd.

"If it comes to anything, the muzhik may falter," he said, "and here we need proletarian determination."

The Bolshevik delegates to the Constituent Assembly, who began arriving from all corners of Russia, were, under Lenin's pressure and Sverdlov's directions, assigned to various factories, workshops, and military centres. They constituted an important element in the organization of the 'supplementary revolution' of January 5th. As to the Social Revolutionary deputies, they considered it incompatible with the high calling of a representative of the nation to take part in any struggle: "The people have elected us—let the people defend us." In truth, these provincial petty bourgeois just did not know what to do with themselves and the majority were simply frightened. But they prepared thoroughly for the whole ceremonial of the first session: they brought candles with them just in case the Bolsheviks cut off the electricity supply, and a large reserve of sandwiches just in case the Bolsheviks deprived them of food.

That was how democracy marched into battle against dictatorship—fully armed with candles and sandwiches. The people, however, did not even give a thought to defending those who considered themselves the nation's representatives, but were, in fact, only faint shadows of an outworn period of the revolution.

During the liquidation of the Constituent Assembly I was in Brest-Litovsk. Soon afterwards, when I returned to Petrograd for some consultation, Lenin commented: "Of course, we took great risks in not adjourning the convocation of the Assembly; of course, we acted very, very imprudently. But in the end it turned out all to the good. By dispersing the Constituent Assembly, the Soviet regime, in the name of proletarian dictatorship, openly and finally put an end to formal democracy . . . This lesson will not be forgotten." That was how theoretical generalization went hand in hand with the practical use of the Latvian infantry regiment. It must have been at that time that Lenin was definitely reaching the conclusions which later, during the first Congress of the Comintern, he so brilliantly formulated in his theses on democracy.

The critique of formal democracy has, as we know, its own long history. The 1848 revolution and its transitory character was regarded by us and by our predecessors as the crumbling of political democracy which was to be followed by 'social' democracy. But bourgeois society knew how to make 'social' democracy take the place which democracy pure and simple could maintain no longer. There was a long period in political history when 'social' democracy, nourished by the critique of pure democracy, in fact differed little from the latter; it took over all the latter's tasks and became permeated with all its vices. Not once in the past has it happened that the opposition was called upon to solve, by conservative means, those problems which the compromised regime of yesterday was unable to solve. From a transitory stage, which was to serve only as a preparatory period for proletarian dictatorship, democracy became the highest criterion, the supreme tribunal, the sacred temple, in essence the acme of hypocrisy of bourgeois society. This was what happened in Russia. Having received a mortal blow in October, the bourgeoisie still tried in January to reincarnate itself in the phantom-like, holy, Constituent Assembly. The victorious developments of the proletarian revolution which followed the open, frank, and brutal dispersal of the Constituent Assembly, gave formal democracy the *coup de grâce* from which it was never to recover. This was why Lenin was right when he remarked: "In the end it all turned out to the good!"

In this Assembly of Social Revolutionaries the February republic had an opportunity to die its second death.

Against the background of the general impressions connected with the official 'February' Russia and with the Petrograd Soviet composed then of Menshevik and Social Revolutionaries, one figure of an SR delegate stands out clearly, as if it were only yesterday. I have no idea who he was, or where he came from, but he must have arrived from the provinces. Outwardly, he looked like a young school teacher from a worthy pedagogical institute: flat-nosed, bespectacled, nearly beardless, with the face of a simpleton, with high cheekbones. I saw him at that session at which the socialist ministers presented themselves for the first time before the Soviet. Chernov, diffusely, eloquently, with sickening flourishes, coquetry and sweet persuasiveness was explaining why he and the others had joined the government and what would be the blessed consequences of this act. I remember particularly one tiresome phrase which the orator kept on repeating dozens of times: "You have pulled us into the government and it is up to you to pull us out." The schoolmaster gazed at the speaker with eyes full of intense admiration. This is how a faithful pilgrim who had reached a famous shrine and is about to hear the homily of a holy man must feel and look. The speech flowed endlessly;

the audience now and again grew tired and there was a slight murmur. But the schoolmaster's sources of veneration seemed to be inexhaustible. "This is what our revolution—or rather *their* revolution—looks like," I said to myself during the session of the Soviets of 1917 to which I listened and which I was watching for the first time. There was loud applause after Chernov finished his speech. Only in one corner a small group of dissatisfied Bolsheviks exchanged their impressions. They came at once to the fore when they supported, in a friendly fashion, my criticism of the 'ministerialism' and the politics of national defence preached by the Mensheviks and the SRs. The reverent schoolmaster was greatly disturbed and frightened. He was not indignant: during those days he dared not yet be angry with an émigré who had returned to his fatherland. But he could not understand how one could be against such a happy and, in all respects admirable event like the entry of Chernov into the provisional government. The young man sat a few steps from me, and on his face, at which I looked as upon a barometer of the meeting, fear and incomprehension struggled with faith as yet unshattered. The image remained with me for ever—it personified the February revolution, or its better aspect: simple, naïve, mediocre, petty bourgeois schoolmasterish; it also had another face, much worse, that of Dan and Chernov.

Not without reason and not by accident, Chernov turned out to be the President of the Constituent Assembly. He was raised up by the February revolution, the still slow-moving, republican revolution of half-Oblomovs,[1] still full of delusions, and oh! how ingenuous in some ways and oh! how artful in others. The drowsy muzhik, through such agents as these devout tutors, was raising up and elevating the Chernovs; Chernov himself was receiving the mandate not without a 'truly Russian' grace and equally 'truly Russian'

---

[1] Oblomov is a character in Goncherov's novel and symbolizes the will-less, indolent, inert Russian nobleman. (Translator's note.)

deceitfulness.[2] What I am trying to say is that Chernov was also in a sense a national type. I am saying that he was *also* a national type, because some four years ago I wrote about Lenin's national characteristics. The juxtaposition, or even an indirect collocation of these two figures may seem incongruous; and it would indeed be foolish and incongruous if we were to link the two personalities. But what I have in mind are 'elemental' national features and the way they become embodied and refract themselves. Chernov is the epigone of the old revolutionary tradition of the intelligentsia; Lenin is at one and the same time its crowning achievement and its complete repudiation. In the old intellectual there lived a nobleman, beating his breast and babbling profusely about his debt to the people; among the old intelligentsia you could find the reverential tutor who lived with his aunt surrounded by icons, and who opened a window—just a slit—into the world of critical thought; there might have also been a nice enlightened peasant hesitating between socialization and the chunk of a farm offered by Stolypin;[3] there might also have been a solitary worker who had rubbed shoulders a little with the gentlemen-students and, as a result, had left his own people but had not become one with the others. All this is represented by 'Chernovism' with its honeyed tongue, its formlessness, mediocre through and through. In the days of Sophia Perovskaya[4] there was idealism among the intellectuals, but of this there was hardly a trace in the world of Chernovs. What had been added had come from the new industrial-

---

[2] Trotsky uses the word *rasseiskoi*, which here is an ironical distortion of the word 'Russian'. (Translator's note.)

[3] Stolypin was the Minister of the Interior, and later Prime Minister in the period of counter-revolutionary terror after the defeat of the 1905 revolution. In November 1906 he decreed an 'agrarian reform' which gave the rich peasant just a little more land. (Translator's note.)

[4] A young member of the *Narodnaya Volya*, took part in the attempt on the life of Tsar Alexander II. Was sentenced to death and executed in April 1881. (Translator's note.)

commercial Russia and is well expressed in the maxim of our traders: "Who does not cheat does not sell."

In his time Herzen was an immense and wonderful influence on the development of Russian thought. But let him outstay his epoch by half a century, deprive him of the gorgeous plumage of his talent, turn him into his own epigone, place him against the background of the years 1905–1917 and here you have an element of 'Chernovism'. It is much more difficult to perform a similar operation with Chernyshevsky; but all the Chernovs have in themselves something of a caricature of Chernyshevsky. The connection with Mikhailovsky[5] is more direct, because Mikhailovsky himself outlived his ideas. Under the surface of the whole of our development, as under the Chernovism, there is the peasant element, refracted in the immature half-educated petty-bourgeoisie of small towns and villages or in the over-ripe and already slightly decaying intelligentsia. The culmination of Chernovism was, of necessity, ephemeral. In February there was a first tremor: the soldier, the worker, and the muzhik woke up; gradually the jolt affected the volunteers in the army, the teachers, the students, the lawyers; then it made itself felt in the 'contact commissions' and other cleverly devised institutions; that shock lifted the Chernovs on to the democratic heights, while in the meantime . . . down below the very foundations had shifted and the democratic peaks were left suspended in the void. That was why between February and October the whole spirit of Chernovism found its expression in the appeal: "Stay awhile —time—you are so beautiful!" But time did not stand still. The devil was taking possession of the soldier; the muzhik began baulking, even the tutor was quickly shedding the reverence of February. In consequence the Chernovs, their robes blown about by the wind, slithered unbecomingly from unimagined heights into the muddy puddles of reality.

[5] N. K. Mikhailovsky (1842–1904), Russian sociologist and journalist, the ideologue of the liberal Populists, was a rabid anti-Marxist. (Translator's note.)

There was a peasant undercurrent in Leninism too, in so far as it exists in our proletariat and runs through the whole of our history. Fortunately, in our history there was not only apathy or the spirit of Oblomov there was action too. Our peasant was full of senseless prejudice, but he was also capable of good sense. All that was action and courage, all that was hatred of oppression and of stagnation, all the contempt for weak characters—in a word, all those features which determine a mass movement formed by a shift in social classes and the dynamics of class struggle found their expression in Bolshevism. The peasant element refracted itself in this case in the proletariat, that is in the most dynamic force in our history and in history at large; and Lenin was the perfect embodiment of that force. Precisely in this sense the peasant-national element was in Lenin raised to the highest point; while in Chernovs the same national feature remained at its lowest.

The tragi-comic episode of January 5th 1918 (the dispersal of the Constituent Assembly) was in principle the last skirmish between Leninism and Chernovism. "In principle", because in reality there was no skirmish at all, only a small and pathetic demonstration of a rearguard of 'democracy', bowing itself off the stage, armed with its candles and sandwiches. All the blown-up illusions collapsed like pricked balloons; all the cheap decorations fell to the ground; all the puffed-up moral strength was revealed in all its half-witted impotence. *Finis.*

6

The Business of Government

I N PETERSBURG power is taken over. The government
has to be formed.

"What shall we call it?" asked Lenin, thinking aloud.
"Only let us not use the word Minister: it is a dull, hack-
neyed title."

"Perhaps 'Commissars'," I suggested, "only there are too
many Commissars just now. Perhaps Supreme Commissars?
. . . No, 'Supreme' sounds wrong too. What about 'People's
Commissars'?"

"People's Commissars? Well, this sounds all right. And
the government as a whole?"

"Council of People's Commissars?"

"Council of People's Commissars," picked up Lenin.
"That's splendid; it smells of revolution."

This last sentence I remember by heart.[1]

Behind the scenes laborious negotiations went on with
Vikzhel (Executive Committee of the Railway Workers'
Union), with the left SRs, and with others. About all this I
have not much to say. I only remember the violent indignation with which Lenin reacted to *Vikzhel*'s insolent demands
and his no less violent indignation against those among us
who were impressed by these demands. However, we continued the negotiations, because for the time being we had
to reckon with *Vikzhel*.

On Comrade Kamenev's initiative, Kerensky's decree

---

[1] T. Miliutin related this episode somewhat differently, but my
version seems to me more correct. In any case, Lenin's words "it
smells of revolution" referred to my suggestion of calling the government as a whole the Council of People's Commissars.

introducing capital punishment for troops was repealed. I do not remember now before which body Kamenev brought his proposal, but it must have been the Military Revolutionary Committee most probably, and he must have done it already on the morning of October 25th (November 7th). I recall that I was present when the proposal was made and that I did not object. Lenin was not there at the time; it must have been before his arrival at the Smolny. When he learned about this first piece of legislation, his anger was unbounded.

"Nonsense," he kept on repeating. "How can one make a revolution without firing squads? Do you think you will be able to deal with all your enemies by laying down your arms? What other means of repression do you have? Imprisonment? To this no one attaches any importance during a civil war when each side hopes to win."

Kamenev tried to prove that the abolished decree was introduced by Kerensky especially against soldier-deserters. But Lenin was adamant. For him it was clear that the abolition of capital punishment resulted from a lack of serious considerations of all the enormous difficulties which we were going to encounter presently.

"It is a mistake," he went on, "an inadmissible weakness, a pacifist illusion," and so on, and so on. He proposed to rescind the decree straightaway. There was opposition and the argument was raised that this would produce a very unfortunate impression. Someone said: "It would be better simply to have recourse to a firing squad when it becomes obvious that there is no other way." The matter ended thus.

The bourgeois newspapers and those of the Social Democrats and the Mensheviks right from the first day of the upheaval kept up a unanimous chorus of wolves, jackals, and rabid dogs. Only the *Novoye Vremya* tried to adopt a 'loyal' tone, tail between hind legs.

"Aren't we going to bridle this rabble?" Lenin kept on asking at every opportunity. "Well, excuse me, what sort of dictatorship is this?"

The newspapers got hold especially of the slogan: "grab

what has been grabbed" and churned it up on all possible occasions, in their leading articles, in their poems, and in their correspondence columns.

"They do stick to that 'grab what has been grabbed'," said Lenin one day in comic despair.

"Whose words were they?" I asked, "or were they just invented?"

"No, somehow I said it myself," answered Lenin. "I said it and then forgot all about it, and they have made of these words a whole political programme." And, discouraged, he waved his hand in jest.

Anyone who knew anything about Lenin was aware that one of his strong points was the ability in every instance to distinguish the essence of the matter from the form. But it might be worthwhile to stress that he also attached importance to the form, realizing how much the formal side of things dominates people's mind; in this way he was able to invest formality with substance. From the moment of the deposition of the Provisional Government, Lenin systematically, in small things as well as in great, acted as a government should. We had not yet any governmental apparatus; our contact with the provinces was non-existent; we were sabotaged by officialdom; *Vikzhel* was interfering with our telegraphic connections with Moscow; we had no money; we had no army. But all the time and everywhere Lenin ruled by decisions, decrees, and orders in the name of the government. It goes without saying that Lenin less than anybody else was inclined to be impressed by the magic of formality. He was acutely conscious of the fact that our strength lay in this new governmental apparatus which was organizing itself from below, from the Petersburg districts. But in order to conduct the work 'from above', from the offices deserted by the saboteurs, in conjunction with the creative work from below, this formal tone was needed, the tone of a government which today is still suspended in a vacuum, but which tomorrow or the day after would become a force, and for this reason already today acts as a force. This formality was also needed in order to discipline our own brethren. The governmental apparatus was slowly spreading its net over the turmoil and ferment, over revolutionary improvisations of advanced proletarian groups.

Lenin's office and my own were situated on the two opposite sides of the Smolny Institute. The corridor which connected, or rather separated, the two rooms was so long that Lenin, jokingly, proposed to establish liaison by means of cyclists. We communicated by telephone; often sailors would be coming in, bringing those extraordinary notes from Lenin; written on small pieces of paper, they contained two or three strongly worded blunt sentences, with the most important passages underlined twice or thrice, and with a final question—also set out bluntly. Several times a day I used to march along the unending corridor, resembling a beehive, to Vladimir Ilyich's office for discussions. In the centre of our preoccupations were military questions. I used to leave the running of the Ministry of Foreign Affairs entirely to Comrades Markin and Zalkind. I limited myself to producing a few notes of a propagandist character and receiving a small number of visitors.

The German offensive was creating the most difficult problems for us and we had no means to resolve them; nor did we have any possibility of finding those means or creating them. We started by an appeal. We discussed my draft, 'Socialist fatherland in danger', together with the left Social Revolutionaries. The SRs, as new converts to internationalism, were bothered by the title of the appeal. Lenin, on the contrary, approved of it:

"It shows immediately that we have made a 180 degree turn as far as the question of national defence is concerned. That is just what is needed."

One of the final paragraphs contained a warning that whoever gave help to the enemy would be put to death on the spot. The left Social Revolutionary, Steinberg—I do not know what queer wind blew him towards the revolution and even right into the Council of People's Commissars—

protested against this cruel threat which, according to him, spoilt the "dramatic effect of the appeal".

"On the contrary!" exclaimed Lenin, "exactly in this resides the genuine revolutionary 'dramatic effect'." (He pronounced the words "dramatic effect" with an ironical twist.) "Do you really think that we shall come out victorious without any revolutionary terror?"

This was the time when Lenin at every suitable opportunity stressed the inevitability of terror. Any signs of sentimentality, of easy-going cordiality, of softness—and there was a great surplus of all this—angered him not by themselves, but because he saw in them proof that even the élite of the working class was not fully aware of all the extraordinarily difficult tasks which could be accomplished only by means of quite extraordinary energy.

"They," he used to say about our enemies, "they run the risk of losing everything. And yet they have hundreds of thousands of men who went through the experience of war, who are well fed, courageous; they have officers, junkers, the sons of landlords and industrialists, sons of policemen and rich peasants, who are ready for anything. And here are those, excuse the word, 'revolutionaries' who imagine that we shall achieve our revolution in a nice way, with kindness? What have they learned? What do they understand by 'dictatorship'? And what sort of a dictatorship will that be if they themselves are ninnies?"

Admonitions of this kind one could hear tens of times daily, and they were always aimed at somebody present who was suspected of 'pacifism'. Lenin would not let an occasion pass—when the talk was about revolution or dictatorship, especially during the meetings of the *Sovnarkom* (Council of People's Commissars) or in the presence of Left SRs or vacillating communists—without remarking: "Where is our dictatorship? Well, show it to me? We have a mess, not a dictatorship." The word 'mess' he liked very much. "If we are incapable of shooting a White Guard saboteur, then what sort of a great revolution is this? Just look what those bourgeois wretches write in their newspapers? Where is the dictatorship? Nothing but prattle and mess. . ."

These exhortations expressed Lenin's real state of mind, but they also had their well-defined purpose: true to his method, Lenin was hammering in the realization that extremely stern measures would be inevitable for the safety of the revolution.

The impotence of the new governmental apparatus became strikingly evident when the Germans went over to the offensive.

"Yesterday we were still firmly in the saddle," said Lenin when we were alone, "and today we are barely holding on to the mane. That is a lesson for us! That will teach us how to get out of our accursed Oblomovism! That will teach us how to introduce order into our affairs, to get to grips with our work as we should if we don't want to remain slaves. Indeed, this will be a lesson for us but only . . . only if the Germans together with the Whites don't manage to bowl us over!"

Once, all of a sudden, Lenin asked:

"And what if the White Guards kill you and me? Will Bukharin and Sverdlov manage on their own?"

"Oh, well . . . they won't kill us," I answered laughing.

"Devil only knows," said Lenin and also laughed. At that the conversation ended.

In one of the halls of the same Smolny Institute the General Staff used to hold their meetings. This was the most disorderly of all establishments. One could never understand who commanded, who issued orders and to whom. Here for the first time was raised, in a general manner, the question of military specialists. In this matter we had already acquired some experience during the struggle against Krasnov[2] when we appointed Colonel Muraviev as commander and he, on his part, entrusted the conduct of the

---

[2] Cossack General Krasnov was a monarchist, who in the last days of October marched together with Kerensky on Petersburg. (Translator's note.)

operations at Pulkovo to Colonel Valden. To Muraviev[3] we assigned four sailors and one soldier, who were instructed to watch both men and not to take their hands off their revolvers. Such were the beginnings of the system of army commissars. This experience proved to a certain extent useful when the Supreme Military Council was set up.

"Without serious and experienced military personnel we shall not manage to overcome the chaos," I kept telling Vladimir Ilyich after each visit to the General Staff.

"Yes, it seems you are right. But how to guard against treachery ... ?"

"We shall assign a commissar to each."

"Let's assign two," exclaimed Lenin, "and tough ones at that. It is impossible that we should not have tough communists."

In this way the Supreme Military Council came into existence.

The transfer of government to Moscow caused a great deal of friction. Some said that this would be abandoning Petrograd which laid the foundations of the revolution; the workers would not understand this; the Smolny had become the symbol of the Soviet regime, and now you propose to liquidate it, and so on, and so forth. Lenin was beside himself with anger:

"How can one by such sentimental nonsense obscure the whole problem of the revolution's future? If the Germans in one big swoop overrun Petersburg—and all of us—then the revolution perishes. If the government is in Moscow, then the fall of Petersburg will be a grievous blow, but only a blow. How is it that you don't see this, that you don't understand? Moreover, in the present conditions, if we remain in Petersburg we are only increasing the military danger; it is as if we were inviting the Germans to take

[3] Colonel Muraviev sympathized with the Left Social Revolutionaries after the uprising; later on tried to pass over to the enemy. In 1918 he died of a bullet shot either from a Bolshevik or from his own hand. (Translator's note.)

Petersburg. If the government is in Moscow, the temptation to seize Petersburg is much smaller: what advantage is there in occupying a hungry revolutionary city if this occupation is not decisive for the fate of the revolution and of peace? Why do you prattle about the symbolic importance of the Smolny! The Smolny is what it is because we are in it. When we are in the Kremlin, all your symbolism will move to the Kremlin."

Finally, the opposition to the move was defeated. The government was transferred to Moscow. I remained for some time in Petrograd as president of the Military Revolutionary Committee, if I am not mistaken. When I went to Moscow, I found Vladimir Ilyich in the Kremlin, in the so-called Cavalry Building. "The mess", that is the chaos and disorder, was just as great here as it had been in the Smolny. Good-humouredly Lenin was scolding the Muscovites preoccupied by questions of hierarchy, and gradually, step by step, was tightening the reins.

The government which in its composition was changing quite often, developed a feverish activity of passing ever new decrees. Every session of the Council of People's Commissars in this period presented a picture of legislative improvisation on a grand scale. Everything was in its beginnings, everything had to be built anew. There was no use looking for 'precedents', because history had not supplied any. There was not even enough time to make simple inquiries. The issues debated were only those which from the revolutionary point of view were most urgent—this contributed to chaos and disorder. Great problems were often mixed up with small ones in a most fantastic manner. Secondary practical issues led to the most complicated questions of principle. Decrees did not always accord with one another, far from it. And Lenin more than once, even publicly, made ironic remarks about the lack of consistency in our creativity in the field of decrees. But in the end, all these contradictions, even those which seemed very sharp when considered from the point of view of the practical tasks of the moment, were permeated by revolutionary thought trying to chart new roads leading to a new order of human relationships.

It goes without saying that the leadership in all this activity was Lenin's. Untiringly, he presided, five or six hours at a stretch, over the meetings of the Council of People's Commissars, which at that period took place every day; he directed the debates passing from subject to subject, severely limiting speakers' time according to his pocket-watch which soon was replaced by a chairman's chronometer. As a rule, the topics of discussion were put on the agenda without any previous preparation, and, as I said before, always demanding extreme urgency. Very often neither the chairman nor the Commissars were familiar with the essentials of a problem until it became the subject of the debate. But the discussion was always concise: for the preliminary exposition of the theme the speaker had no more than five to ten minutes, and yet the chairman somehow gropingly always found the right line along which to steer the debate. When there was a meeting at which many people were present, among them specialists or people unknown to Lenin, he resorted to his favourite gesture: he would put his right hand over his forehead and eyes and look through between his stretched fingers. Thus, playing peep-bo, he observed the speaker and the participants very intently and attentively and saw exactly what he needed to see. On narrow strips of paper, in small writing (economy measures!) he noted the names of the speakers. He kept one eye on the watch which now and again appeared over the table to remind the orator that the time was up. Meanwhile, he quickly jotted down the essential conclusions resulting from the debate. In addition, in order to save time, he was sending out to some participants short notes in which he asked for particular information.

These notes would have constituted a rich and important epistolary documentation on the technique of Soviet legislation. Most of them, unfortunately, were lost, if only because the answer was usually written on the reverse side of the paper and on receiving it the chairman straightway crumpled it up or tore it to bits. Then at a certain moment Lenin would read the salient points of the resolution, always expressed in a dry style and with a didactic lucidity, so that all should be stressed, clear, and unlikely to lead to confusion. After that the discussion was either brought to an end or devoted to some practical issues or to some supplementary elucidation. Lenin's 'points' formed the basis of a decree. To conduct this kind of work one needed, apart from other qualities, an immense creative imagination.

The word 'imagination' may, at first glance, seem inappropriate in this context, and yet it expresses the very essence of the thing. There are various aspects of imagination: an engineer-designer needs imagination just as much as a bohemian romantic. One of the most valuable attributes of imagination is its ability to conceive of people, things, and phenomena as they really are, although one might never have had a chance to observe them. The ability to make use of one's experience and theoretical principles, to coordinate disparate hints and pieces of information which are, so to speak, in the air, and assimilate them, to supplement them, unite them together according to some unformulated laws of harmony, and, in this way, to reconstitute in all its concrete reality a field of human existence—this is the kind of imagination so indispensable to any legislator, administrator, or leader, especially in a revolutionary epoch. Lenin's strength lay, in great measure, in the richness of his realistic imagination. The tense and concentrated manner in which he was pursuing his aim had always in it this element of concreteness, of reality; otherwise it would never have been so purposeful.

Lenin himself, in the *Iskra*, I think, expressed for the first time the idea that in the complex chain of political acts one had to be able, at a given moment, to discern the main, the central, link in order to seize it and to impart to the whole chain the desired direction. More than once Lenin used to return to this conception and even to the metaphor. From his conscious mind this methodological notion seemed to have permeated into his subconscious and in the end it became as if his second nature. During the most critical periods, when he was faced with tactical decisions involving a high degree of risk or exceptional responsibility, Lenin was able to set aside all that was irrelevant, all that was secondary, all that was inessential and that could be deferred. This does not mean that he considered only the main, the central part of his task, ignoring the details. On the contrary, he viewed the problem with which he had to come to grips in all its concrete reality, approaching it from every side, weighing all its details, sometimes even tertiary ones, searching for ever new points of attack, trying to find new ways of exercising pressure, of checking facts, and calling for action. But in all this he would never lose sight of 'the link', which at that particular moment he thought was of decisive importance. He brushed aside not only everything directly or indirectly in conflict with the job in hand, but also everything which might disperse attention or slacken tension. In the most critical moments he became as if deaf and blind to all that went beyond the cardinal problem which absorbed him. In the mere posing of other questions, 'neutral ones', he saw a danger from which he instinctively recoiled. Later on, when the critical hurdle was happily cleared, Lenin would still now and again exclaim: "And yet we quite forgot to do this or that. . ." Or "we missed an opportunity because we were so preoccupied by the main thing. . ." Someone would answer him: "But this question had been posed, and this proposal had been made, only you did not want to hear anything!"

"Didn't I? Impossible!" he would say, "and I don't remember a thing."

At that point he would burst out laughing, with malicious laughter in which there was an admission of 'guilt'; and he would make a characteristic gesture of raising his arm and moving it helplessly down, as if resigned: well, one cannot do everything. This 'shortcoming' of his was only the obverse side of his talent to mobilize, to the utmost degree, all his inner forces. Precisely this talent made of him the greatest revolutionary in history.

In his theses on peace, written at the beginning of January 1918, Lenin says that "for its success socialism in Russia needs a certain spell of time, *at least a few months*." These words seem absolutely incomprehensible now: wasn't this a slip of the pen? Did he not mean "a few years" or "a few decades"? No, this was no slip. One could probably find quite a number of statements of this kind. I very well remember how, in the first period, in the Smolny, Lenin at the session of the Sovnarkom repeatedly said that in half a year we would have socialism and would become one of the most powerful states. Not only the left Social Revolutionaries used to raise their eyebrows questioningly and, in surprise, glance at each other, but keep silent. This was Lenin's 'method of persuasion'. This was his way of teaching people around him to consider all problems from the viewpoint of socialist construction—not in the long perspective of the 'final aim', but in the immediate perspective of today and tomorrow. And here, in this sudden transition, he had recourse to a mode peculiarly his own—a certain exaggeration: yesterday we maintained that socialism is the 'final aim', today we have to think, talk, and act in such a manner as to secure the socialist order in a few months. Was this then a didactic trick only? No, not just a trick. There was something more to Lenin's pedagogical firmness: there was the force of his idealism and the tenacity of his indomitable will which at the sharp turns of history made him cut corners and fore-shorten distances. *He believed in what he was saying.* And so the fantastic date for socialism—six months hence—testi-fied also to the same Leninist spirit which showed itself in his realistic approach to every immediate task. The deep and unyielding conviction that there were tremendous possibili-ties of human development for which one could, one should, pay the price of suffering and sacrifice, was always the hall-mark of Leninism.

In the most difficult circumstances, in the course of the most wearing daily tasks, amid shortages of food and all other disasters, in the heat of the civil war, Lenin assiduously worked on the elaboration of the Soviet Constitution, endeavouring scrupulously to achieve a balance between the secondary and tertiary needs of the state apparatus and the fundamental tasks of the proletarian dictatorship in a peasant country.

The Constitutional Commission decided, for some reasons, to revise Lenin's 'Declaration of the Rights of the Toilers' so that it should 'accord' somehow with the Constitution. When I returned from the front to Moscow, I received the text of this revised 'Declaration', or, in any case, a part of it. I was looking through all these materials in Lenin's office, in his and Sverdlov's presence. We were in the process of preparing the Fifth Congress of the Soviets.

"Why, in fact, should the 'Declaration' be revised?" I asked Sverdlov who directed the work of the Constitutional Commission.

Vladimir Ilyich, interested, raised his head.

"Well, the Commission found that there are discrepancies and inexact formulations between the text of the Declaration and the text of the Constitution," answered Yakov Mikhailovich.

"In my view the Commission was wrong," I said, "The Declaration was adopted and became a historical document —what is the sense in revising it?"

"Quite right," interjected Vladimir Ilyich. "In my opinion all this was quite useless. Let this nursling live, untidy and unkempt as it is; still, it is the child of the revolution. . . Will it be any better after a visit to the hairdresser?"

Sverdlov out of a sense of duty at first tried to defend the action of the Commission, but soon he agreed with us. I understood that Vladimir Ilyich, who more than once had to oppose this or that proposal of the Constitutional Commission, did not want to take up the struggle about the wording of the 'Declaration' of which he was the author. He was, nevertheless, extremely pleased that he found the support of a 'third party' turning up unexpectedly in the nick of time. We agreed, all three of us, not to revise the Declaration and the wonderful baby was spared the solicitude of a hairdresser. . .

The study of Soviet legislation and its evolution, with particular attention to the main turning points connected with the course of the revolution itself, and with the class relationship of society, is an immensely important task, because conclusions drawn from it may be, and should be, of great practical significance.

The collection of Soviet decrees forms in a certain sense a part, and not a negligible part, of the Complete Works of Vladimir Ilyich Lenin.

7

The Czechoslovaks and the Left Social Revolutionaries

THE SPRING of 1918 was very hard indeed. Sometimes one had the feeling that everything was slipping away, going to pieces, that there was nothing to hold on to, nothing to lean on. On the one hand it was quite obvious that had it not been for the October upheaval, the country would have fallen into decay. On the other, in the spring of 1918 one had to pose the question: Will this country, so exhausted, so ruined, and so desperate, have enough vitality to support the new regime? There were no supplies. There was no army. The governmental machinery was just beginning to be organized. Plots and conspiracies were spreading like festering sores. The Czechoslovak army on our soil behaved like an independent power; we could do nothing, or nearly nothing, to oppose it.

Once, in those terrible days of 1918, Vladimir Ilyich said to me:

"Today I received a delegation of workers.[1] I talked to them and then one man said: 'We can see that you, Comrade Lenin, are also taking the side of the capitalists.' You know, it was the first time that I heard such words. And I must admit, I was so taken aback that I did not know what to answer. If this was not just a wicked man and not a Menshevik, then here is an alarming symptom."

Relating this episode to me Lenin seemed to be more depressed and shaken than he was when, later on, bad news

---

[1] I very much regret that I cannot remember what the business of that delegation was.

was coming from the front about the fall of Kazan or about a direct military threat to Petersburg. This was understandable: Kazan and even Petersburg could have been lost and then regained, but the trust of the workers constitutes the real, the fundamental capital of the party.

"I have the impression," I told Vladimir Ilyich then, "that the country, like a patient emerging from grave illnesses, is now in need of solid nourishment, of peace, of attention and care, in order to survive and recover; a slight shock may be fatal."

"Yes, this is my impression too," agreed Lenin. "Such frightening anaemia! Now any concussion is dangerous."

And just then the whole business of the Czechoslovak troops threatened to produce the dangerous shock. This foreign army spread like a tumour into the limp flesh of south-eastern Russia, meeting no resistance, and growing bigger with the accretion of the Social Revolutionaries and other activists of an even whiter hue. Although power was already in Bolshevik hands everywhere, there was still considerable disarray in the provinces. No wonder. It was only in Petersburg and in Moscow that the revolution had been really carried through; in the majority of the provincial cities the October Revolution, like the February one, was carried, so to speak, over the telegraph poles. Here in some places they were linked, in others they were not, just because things were happening in the capital. The formlessness of the social environment, the lack of resistance on the part of the former masters found its reflection in a certain formlessness on the revolutionary side. The appearance on the scene of the Czechoslovak batallions modified the situation, first to our disadvantage but in the end in our favour. The Whites found a military centre around which to rally. But in return the Reds began in all seriousness to rally their own revolutionary forces as well. One could say that it was only with the arrival of the Czechoslovak troops that the people of the Volga region made their October revolution. But it was not to be accomplished in a day.

On July 3rd Vladimir Ilyich phoned me at the Commissariat of War.

"Do you know what has happened?" he said in that muffled voice which with him usually was a sign of some agitation.

"No, what is it?"

"The left SRs threw a bomb at Mirbach; apparently he is gravely wounded. Come straight to the Kremlin, we have to discuss the matter."

A few minutes later I was in Lenin's office. He told me exactly what had happened, and at the same time kept asking over the phone for more details.

"What an affair!" I exclaimed, trying to digest this far from ordinary piece of news. "We cannot complain that life is dull."

"Yes, yes," answered Lenin laughing nervously. "That's it—the monstrous convulsion of a petty bourgeois. . ."

There was irony in his voice when he said *"convulsion"*. Engels described the same phenomenon as *der rabiat gewordene Kleinbürger*[2]—"the petty bourgeois gone berserk."

Hurried telephone conversations—brief questions, brief answers—with the Commissariat of Foreign Affairs, with the Department of Home Security (*Cheka*), and other offices. Lenin's thought, as always in critical moments, ran on two planes simultaneously: the Marxist was enriching his historical experience by observing with interest the new frenzy—"the convulsion"—of petty bourgeois radicalism; and the leader of the revolution, tirelessly gathering in his hands all the threads of the affair, was deciding what the next practical steps should be. There were rumours of mutiny among the troops of the Home Security department.

"Well, well, I hope the left SRs will not turn out to be the banana skin on which we shall be destined to slip. . ."

"I just had the very same idea," answered Lenin. "Wouldn't this be precisely the role of the vacillating petty-

---

[2] In German in the text.

bourgeois: to serve as the banana skin which the White Guards so much wish to throw under our feet . . . ? Now we must at any price exercise our influence on the manner in which the Germans will inform Berlin about what has happened. There is more than enough reason for military intervention, especially if one takes into account the fact that Mirbach, no doubt, must have been reporting all the time that we are weak and that the slightest shock would hurt us badly. . ."

Soon Sverdlov arrived—he was the same as always.

"Oh, well," he said greeting me with a smile, "it looks as if we had to change the Council of People's Commissars into a Military Revolutionary Committee once more."

Lenin still continued to collect information. At that moment, or perhaps a little later, came the news of Mirbach's death. Now we had to go to the embassy to pay our 'condolences'. It was decided that Lenin should go with Sverdlov and Chicherin, I think. The question arose whether I should also accompany them.

After a brief exchange of views, they exempted me from that chore.

"How does one express 'condolences'?" asked Vladimir Ilyich shaking his head. "I have already talked to Radek about this. I wanted to say '*Mitleid*', but apparently one has to say '*Beileid*'." With a little chuckle he put on his coat and said firmly to Sverdlov: "Let's go." His expression changed: now he had a greyish stony look. To drive to the Hohenzollern embassy with expressions of sympathy because of Count Mirbach's death was not an easy thing for Vladimir Ilyich to do. It must have been, emotionally, one of the hardest moments in his life.

It is in such situations that one can judge people. Sverdlov was really incomparable: self-confident, resolute, and resourceful: the best type of a Bolshevik. Lenin got to know and appreciate Sverdlov fully precisely during these difficult months. More than once it would happen that Lenin would phone Sverdlov in order to suggest some urgent course of action only to receive the answer: "It has already been done." We often joked about this, saying: "Surely, with Sverdlov it is *already*!"

"Think only, at the beginning we were opposed to his entering the Central Committee," Lenin was recalling. "To what an extent we under-estimated this man."

Sverdlov was indeed the subject of many discussions, but our view of him was corrected 'from below'—by the Congress—and the Congress proved right.[3]

With the revolt of the left Social Revolutionaries we lost a political ally; but in the last analysis this fact only strengthened our position. The Party became more united. In many organizations and in the army the importance of communist cells became better understood. The government's line became firmer. Undoubtedly, the Czechoslovak uprising had a similar effect. It shook the party out of its depression, so widespread since the Brest-Litovsk peace. This was the period of mobilization of party members for the Eastern Front. The first contingent, which still contained the left Social Revolutionaries, had already been sent out by Lenin and myself. In a rather vague form here were the beginnings of the future organization of political sections. However, news from the Volga region continued to be bad. The treachery of Muraviev and the mutiny of the left Social Revolutionaries caused confusion on the Eastern Front. At

---

[3] Sverdlov is generally regarded as the *first* President of the Central Executive Committee after October. This is not correct. The first President was Kamenev, though he had held this post for a short time only. Sverdlov replaced him on Lenin's initiative when, in connection with some attempts at achieving an alliance with the socialist parties, the inner party struggle became sharper. In the notes attached to volume XIV of Lenin's *Works* it is alleged that the substitution of Kamenev by Sverdlov was caused by Kamenev's departure for Brest-Litovsk. This is not true. As I said above, the change came as a result of the sharpening of inner-party controversy. I remember this all the more clearly because I myself was instructed by the Central Committee, at the meeting of the Executive Committee, to put forward Sverdlov's candidature for the post of the President.

once the danger became grave. It was then that a radical change took place.

"Everybody and everything must be mobilized and sent to the front," said Lenin. "Take off from the 'curtain' all regiments half-way fit to fight and direct them to the Volga districts."

I should perhaps explain that we used to call the 'curtain' the thin cordon of troops stationed in the West and facing the territories under German occupation.

"But what about the Germans?"

"The Germans will not budge," answered Lenin, "they won't bother, because it is also in their interest that we should finish with the Czechoslovaks."

This plan was accepted. The regiments sent to the Volga became the nucleus of the future Fifth Army. At the same time it was decided that I should also proceed to the East. I began to organize my military train which was not an easy task then. Vladimir Ilyich too became preoccupied with all the details of this matter: he was sending little notes to me and kept on telephoning.

"Do you have a solid car? Take one from the Kremlin garage."

Then half an hour later:

"Are you taking a plane? You should have a plane, it might come in useful."

"There would be planes attached to the army. If it becomes necessary I may use one," I answered.

Then half an hour later:

"My opinion is, however, that you should have a plane on your train. One never knows what might happen," and so on, and so on.

Our regiments and divisions, hastily assembled from what remained of the old dispersed army, were, as it is known, lamentably scattered at the first encounter with the Czechoslovak troops.

"In order to overcome this alarming lack of stability we need a strong defence cordon formed by communists and shock troops," I said to Lenin before my departure. "We must *force* people to fight. If we wait until the muzhik is fully awake and becomes alert, it may be too late."

"Of course, you are right," he would answer, "but I fear that even the defence cordon may not react with the required strength. The Russian is tender-hearted and incapable of adopting resolute measures of counter-revolutionary terror. And yet we shall have to try."

It was in Sviazhsk that I learned about the attempt on Lenin's life and about the death of Uritsky.[4] These were the tragic days of revolution's internal crisis. The revolution was doing away with its 'tender heart'. The sword of the party was becoming at last steeled. Determination was hardening and when necessary even ruthlessness was not lacking. At the front, the political sections together with the detachments of defence and the tribunals were turning the flabby flesh of the young army into muscles and sinew. Soon the change became evident. We retook Kazan and Simbirsk. In Kazan I received a telegram from Lenin, who was recovering from his wound, congratulating us on our first victories in the Volga region.

Soon afterwards, when I came to Moscow for a short visit, we went, together with Sverdlov, to see Vladimir Ilyich in Gorki. He was recovering quickly, but had not returned yet to work in the capital. We found him in excellent spirits. He wanted to know all the details about the organization of the army, about the morale of the troops, about the activity of the communists, about the improvement in discipline. He kept on exclaiming: "That's good! That's splendid! The consolidation of the army will soon have its effect on the whole country—everywhere discipline will improve and with it the sense of responsibility."

And indeed already at the beginning of autumn one

---

[4] M. S. Uritsky, member of Trotsky's Inter-Borough Organization, joined the Bolsheviks in 1917. In 1918 he was killed by the S.Rs. (Translator's note.)

noticed the great change. Of that bloodless debility so evident in the spring there was no more trace. Something had moved, had put on strength; and it was remarkable that this time not a feeling of respite, but, on the contrary, of new acute danger saved the revolution by bringing to the surface all the hidden resources of the proletariat's revolutionary energy. When we were getting into the car, Lenin stood gay and cheerful on the balcony. I had seen him so cheerful only on October 25th, when in the Smolny he learned about the first military victories of the uprising.

Politically, we finished off the left Social Revolutionaries. We proceeded with the mopping-up operations on the Volga. Lenin recovered from his wound. The revolution grew in power and vigour.

8
Lenin on the Rostrum

SINCE THE October Revolution Lenin has been photographed more than once; he has also been filmed; his voice has been recorded; his speeches taken down in shorthand and printed. Thus we have all the elements of his personality—but only the elements, while the living personality itself consists in their unique and always dynamic combination.

When I try to recall to my mind, to see once again with a fresh eye and to hear with a fresh ear, the first occasion on which I saw and heard Lenin on the platform, I see in front of me a solidly built man, a sturdy, supple figure of medium height; I hear an even-flowing smooth voice with slightly rolling r's, speaking fast, almost without pauses and, at the beginning, without any particular intonation.

His first sentences usually about generalities: the speaker probing his audience; the proper balance not yet achieved, his gesture uncertain, his gaze seemingly turned inward; the face rather sullen and even morose—his thoughts working out the way of approach to the audience. The introductory period takes more or less time according to the kind of audience, the subject matter, and the mood of the speaker. Then he finds his right tone. The outlines of the theme become clear. The speaker bends the upper part of the body, sticks his thumbs into the armholes of his waistcoat. These gestures at once swing out head and elbows. The head by itself does not seem exceedingly large on the sturdy and strong body, well built and balanced. What seems enormous is the forehead and the visibly protruding lumps on the skull. He moves his arms about—neither nervously nor in an exaggerated manner. His hand is broad, with short fingers, 'plebeian', strong. Like the whole figure, it betokens benevolence and kindliness coupled with strength. All this becomes noticeable when the speaker has had the time to warm up. This comes as soon as he sees through his opponents' craftiness or when he himself manages to lead them into a trap. Then, from under the powerful brow Lenin's eyes shine— something of this expression is conveyed by an excellent photograph taken in 1919.

Even the least interested listener, catching that look, pricks his ears up and waits for what is to follow. The high cheekbones glow and seem softened by indulgence and sagacity, behind which one can gauge the keen understanding of men, of social relations, of circumstances, an understanding which reaches the very depths of things. The lower part of the face, with the reddish-greyish beard remains somewhat in the shade. The voice becomes softer, mellower, and at times slyly persuasive.

Then the speaker deals with the supposed objections of his opponent or quotes a malicious sentence from the enemy's writings. Even before he analyses the hostile idea, he gives you to understand that it is without foundation, superficial, wrong. He pulls his thumbs out of his waistcoat, throws his body gently backwards, takes a few short steps back as if clearing the space for an assault, shrugs his thick-set shoulders either with irony or with despair, and stretches his arms expressively, spreading his palms and fingers.

Condemnation, or derision, or humiliation of the opponent—according to who he is and what his case may be— always comes before the refutation of his idea. The listener is given some notice of what to expect and for what to prepare himself mentally. Then begins the logical offensive. The left hand moves again towards the armhole of the waistcoat, or, even more often, into the trouser-pocket. The right hand follows the path and the rhythm of the argument; the left comes to its assistance when needed. The speaker leans towards the audience, moves to the edge of the platform, bends forward, and with a circular motion of his hands, works over his own verbal material. This signifies that we have reached the heart of the matter, the central point of the whole speech.

If there are opponents in the hall, from time to time hostile and critical remarks can be heard. In nine cases out of ten heckling remains unanswered. The speaker says what he has to say, to people to whom he wishes to say it and in a manner which he thinks proper. He does not like to deviate from his trend of thought for the sake of casual repartee. Quick rejoinders are incompatible with his mental concentration. After hostile interruptions his voice becomes harsher, his argument even more strongly focused and more condensed, his thought sharper and his gestures more abrupt. He pays attention to the interruption of an opponent only when it in some way follows his own trend of thought and may help to reach his conclusion more quickly. In such cases his retorts are sometimes quite unexpected because of their deadly simplicity. He lays bare a situation when all his opponents believe he is going to conceal it. Such was more than once the experience of the Mensheviks in the first period of the revolution when they accused Bolshevism of violating democracy and when these accusations still had some freshness.

"Our newspapers have been closed down!"

"Of course, unfortunately not yet all of them. We shall close them all down. (Stormy applause.) The proletarian dictatorship will destroy the very roots of the disgraceful commerce in bourgeois opium." (Stormy applause.)

The speaker stands erect, his hands in his trouser-pockets. There is no trace of posturing, not a tinge of rhetorical inflections in his voice, but in the whole figure, in the position of the head, in the tight lips, the high cheekbones, the slightly hoarse voice there is unshaken confidence in the correctness of his acts and the justice of his cause: "If you want to fight, then let us fight properly!"

When the speaker attacks not the enemy but his own

people, his tone of voice and his gestures are different. In such a case the most violent attack still appeals to 'reason'. Sometimes the voice of the speaker breaks on a high note: this happens when he crossly denounces some of his comrades, to shame them, to show that they have understood absolutely nothing, that they are incapable of producing the slightest argument against him, or that there is not the smallest basis for their objections. Just when he says "the slightest" or "the smallest", his voice breaks into a falsetto, and then the most furious tirade acquires an unexpected shade of benevolence.

The speaker had worked out his idea to the end, to the last practical conclusion: his idea—yes, but not its exposition, not the form, except perhaps for a few telling, most pithy, terse, and colourful expressions, which enter the political life of the party and the country and become the jingling currency accepted everywhere. The construction of his sentences is generally top-heavy, with one proposition loaded on another or leading to another. Such a style of speaking presents stenographers—and editors too—with a hard task. But a line of intense and powerful thought cuts its way surely and clearly through these cumbrous phrases.

Is the speaker really a profoundly educated Marxist, thoroughly versed in economic theory, a man of enormous erudition? It seems, now and again rather, that here is a self-educated man who has arrived at an extraordinary degree of understanding all by himself, by an effort of his own brain, without any scientific apparatus, any scientific terminology, and now expounds it all in his own manner. How is it that we get such an impression? Because the speaker has thought out things not only for himself, but also for the broad masses; because his own ideas have been filtered through the experiences of these masses and in the process have become free of theoretical ballast. He can now construct his own exposition of problems without the scientific scaffolding which served him so well when he approached them first himself.

Sometimes, however, the speaker runs up the stairs of his thought too quickly, taking two or three steps at a bound; this happens when the conclusion seems to him too obvious, too plain and he wants to arrive at it without any further delay.

But, suddenly, he feels that the listeners don't follow him, that the link between him and the audience has snapped. Then he pulls himself together, leaps down and starts his ascent again, but this time more deliberately, in more measured steps. Even his voice changes: it sheds its excessive tenseness and acquires a compellingly persuasive tone. This 'backward leap' of course upsets the whole construction of the discourse. But does one deliver a discourse for the pleasure taken in its construction? Is there any logic more valuable in a political speech than that of a call to action?

When the speaker once more approaches his conclusions, but this time carrying his audience with him without losing anybody on the way, one detects in the hall something like a physical sensation of that well-being and joy which come with a harmonious development of collective thought. Now it only remains to nail the conclusion twice or thrice, so that it holds well, to give it simple, but telling and colourful expression so that it engraves itself on the memory, and then one can afford to give oneself and the listeners a breathing space, to joke and to laugh; in the meantime the collective mind will all the better absorb the newly acquired conclusion.

Lenin's oratorical humour is as plain as all his other artifices, if one can so describe them. In his speeches there are no self-satisfying witticisms, no clever play upon words. His jokes are plain and pithy, intelligible to the masses—they are truly popular. If the political situation gives rise to no anxiety, if the audience consists mostly of 'our own people', the speaker is not averse from occasional jocularity. The audience gratefully receives a naïve and simple jest or a jovially malicious characterization, feeling that it is there not just for the fun of it, but that it has some meaning and purpose and serves the same goal.

When the speaker makes a joke, the lower part of his face

becomes more clearly visible, especially his mouth, with its contagious laughter. The lines of his forehead and skull become softer, the eyes, less piercing, beam cheerfully, the rolling r's become more pronounced; the tension of the concentrated thought relaxes into good-humoured happy laughter.

Lenin's speeches are characterized by what is so essential in all his activity: the intentness on the goal, his purposefulness. The speaker is not out to deliver an oration, but to guide towards a conclusion which is to be followed by action. He has different ways of approaching his audience: he explains; he convinces; he shames it; he jokes with it; and then again tries to convince it and again expounds his idea.

What makes for the unity of his speech is not a preconceived formal plan, but a practical aim, clearly defined and valid for that particular moment, which the audience must take in and absorb into its consciousness. Even the humour has to serve that purpose. The jests themselves are utilitarian. A racy word has its practical significance: it has to stir some and curb others. This is why so many of the expressions coined by Lenin have entered into our political vocabulary.[1] Before he coins such a word, the speaker seems to go round and round as if searching for some central point. Then he finds it and as if placing a nail in position, glances round once more, lifts his hammer with great vigour and hits it on the head once, twice, three times, ten times, until the nail holds firmly, so firmly that it is hard to pull out even when no longer needed. When it is needed no longer, Lenin knocks it from the left, from the right, loosens it, draws it out, jokingly throws it on the pile of scrap-iron in the archives to the great regret of all those who have grown so much accustomed to it.

---

[1] Trotsky quotes here words like *khvostism*—lagging behind; *peredyshka*—breathing spell; *smychka*—concord, harmony, mostly between the economy of the countryside and that of the town; *drachka*—a squabble, a brawl; *komchvanstvo*—communist boastfulness. (Translator's note.)

The speech is coming to an end. The balance sheet is drawn, the conclusions firmly grasped. The speaker looks like a workman who has sweated over his job, but has finished it. From time to time he passes his hand over the bald head on which can be seen little beads of perspiration. The voice becomes muffled—like embers burning in a dying fire. This is the end. But one must not expect any brilliant crowning *finale* without which, one assumes, no speaker can leave the rostrum. Others cannot, but Lenin can. There is no rhetorical winding up: he finishes the sentence and—full stop. Sometimes his final sentence goes thus: "If we understand this, if we do that, then we are sure to vanquish"; or "That is what we should aim at, not in words but in deeds." Or, even more simply, "That is all I wanted to tell you." Such an ending, which accords well with the nature of Lenin's oratory and, generally, with his whole character, does not seem to dampen the enthusiasm of the audience. On the contrary. Precisely after an ending so grey and without effects, the crowd suddenly becomes aware once again of all that Lenin gave it in his speech, and bursts into stormy applause, grateful and enthusiastic.

But Lenin, already gathering his papers, hurriedly leaves the rostrum in order to escape the inevitable. His head withdrawn slightly into his shoulders, chin down, eyes hidden under the brows, his moustache bristling a little crossly on the upper lip pouting with annoyance. The roar of clapping grows, wave upon wave: "Long live . . . Lenin . . . leader . . . Ilyich. . ." Under the glow of electric lamps passes that unique head, surrounded on all sides by waves and waves of enthusiasm. And when it seems the storm has reached its zenith, breaking through the tumult and the clapping, a young voice, strained and happy can be heard: "*Long live Lenin!*" Somewhere, from the inner depths of solidarity, of love, and enthusiasm, like a powerful hurricane there rises a tremendous cry, the call of the people shaking the vaults: "Long live Lenin!"

9

Lenin's National Characteristics[1]

L ENIN'S internationalism does not need to be stressed.
It found striking expression from the first days of the
world war in his irreconcilable break with the counterfeit internationalism which dominated the Second International. The official leaders of 'socialism' tried, from the
height of the parliamentary rostrum, to reconcile the interests
of the fatherland with those of mankind, using abstract
arguments in the style of old-time cosmopolitans. In practice,
as we know, this led to supporting the rapacious fatherland
with the forces of the proletariat.

Lenin's internationalism is not a formula for harmonizing
national and international interests in empty verbiage. It is a
guide to revolutionary action embracing all nations. Our
planet, inhabited by so-called civilized humanity, is considered as one single battlefield where various nations and
social classes contend. The framework of one nation cannot
contain in itself a single weighty problem: visible and
invisible threads connect its very essence with dozens of
events taking place in all corners of the world. In the evalua-
tion of international phenomena and international forces,
Lenin more than anybody else is free from the slightest
national bias.

Marx maintained that the philosophers have sufficiently
interpreted the world; now the real task was to change it.
He, the prophetic genius, did not live to see this fulfilled.
The process of transformation of the old world is now in full

---

[1] On the occasion of Lenin's fiftieth anniversary. *Pravda*, April
23rd, 1920.

swing, and Lenin is its first agent. His internationalism consists in the practical appreciation of, and in the practical intervention in, historic events on a world scale and towards goals which embrace the whole world. Russia and her fate constitute only one element of a tremendous historical process, the outcome of which will decide the fate of humanity.

No, there is no need to authenticate Lenin's internationalism. And yet Lenin himself is a genuinely national type. He is deeply rooted in contemporary Russian history: he is the epitome of that history; he gives it the highest expression and precisely in this way he attains the pinnacle of international activity and of world influence.

To characterize Lenin's personality as 'national' may seem at first sight unexpected; but on closer scrutiny it becomes self-evident. In order to be able to direct an upheaval on a scale unprecedented in the history of nations, the upheaval through which Russia has been passing, there needs to exist between the vital forces of the country and the leader some organic, indissoluble link deep down, at the roots of his being. In himself Lenin embodies the Russian proletariat, politically a young social class which in age is scarcely older than Lenin himself. But that class is deeply national because all Russia's previous and her future development are bound up with it and on it depends the life and death of the Russian nation. Freedom from habit and custom, from hypocrisy and convention, boldness of thought, audacity in action—audacity which never becomes recklessness is characteristic of the Russian proletariat, and of Lenin as well.

These qualities of the Russian proletariat, which actually made of it the most important force of international revolution, had arisen as a result of the whole course of Russian history, of the barbaric cruelty of autocracy, of the feebleness of the privileged classes, of the fitful development of capitalism in dependence on the world stock exchanges, of the hollowness of the Russian bourgeoisie with its decadent ideology and political mediocrity. Our 'Third Estate' did not and could not go through its Reformation or its Great

Revolution; so it became the destiny of the proletariat to confront all-embracing universal revolutionary tasks. Our history never produced a Luther, a Thomas Münzer, nor a Mirabeau, a Danton, or Robespierre. And this was precisely why the Russian proletariat had its Lenin. What was lacking in tradition was amply made up in the scale and sweep of the revolution.

Lenin reflects and represents the working class not only in its proletarian present-day character, but also in its recent peasant past. This indisputable leader of the proletariat had not only the outward look of a muzhik, but he was one too in his innermost being. Outside the Smolny Institute a monument has been erected to another great figure of the world proletariat: Karl Marx stands there on a plinth of stone in a black frock coat. This is only a detail, of course, but even in one's imagination it is impossible to put Lenin into a black frock coat. On some portraits Marx is shown wearing some kind of white starched shirtfront on which dangles something like a monocle. That Marx was not inclined to foppishness is all too obvious to anybody who has the slightest idea of his work. But he was born and grew up in a different national-cultural background, he breathed a different air, as did other leading figures of the German working class, rooted not in peasant villages, but in guilds and corporations and in an elaborate urban culture following upon the Middle Ages.

The very style of Marx, rich and brilliant, combining vigour and flexibility, anger and irony, austerity and sophistication, is marked by all the literary and aesthetic heritage of German political and social writings which go back to the Reformation and beyond. Lenin's literary and oratorical style is extremely simple, utilitarian, spare, as is his whole nature. But in this powerful asceticism there is not a trace of moralizing. This is not a matter of principle, nor a preconceived and worked out system, nor is it, of course, posturing. It is simply the outward expression of an inner concentration of forces, a concentration for action. It is the practical husbandry of a muzhik—only on an immense scale.

The whole of Marx can be found in *The Communist Manifesto*, in the preface to his *Critique*, in *Das Kapital*. Even if he were not the founder of the First International, he would for ever remain what he had been till now. Not so Lenin, whose whole personality is centred in revolutionary action. His scientific works were only the preliminaries to action. If he had never had published a single book, he would for ever have entered history just as he had entered it now: as a leader of the proletarian revolution, a founder of the Third International.

A clear and scientific system, dialectical materialism, was indispensable for the historical sweep of his action; it was indispensable, but it was not sufficient. What was needed too was that deep creative force which we call intuition: the ability to judge events rapidly, at a glance, to distinguish the essential from the trivial, to fill up imaginatively the missing parts of the picture, to think out other people's thoughts to the end, and in the first instance the enemy's thoughts; to combine all these disparate elements into one totality and to strike a blow straightway while the very 'idea' of the blow was still shaping itself in one's mind. This is the intuition of action. This is what we call in Russian true sagacity.

When Lenin, screwing up his left eye, listens over the radio to a parliamentary speech by one of the imperialist politicians, or to a text of a diplomatic note of immediate interest, a note in which bloody perfidy vies with the most affable hypocrisy, he looks like a shrewd muzhik not to be taken in by smooth words and fooled by polite phrases. Such is the sagacity of the peasant, but in this case heightened to a supreme degree, reaching the peak of greatness and armed with all the latest achievements of scientific thought.

The young Russian proletariat could accomplish its tremendous deed only by dragging along with it the peasantry, that heavy lump of rural Russia's sodden earth, stuck fast to its roots. Our national past was leading up to this. But just because history pushed the proletariat to power, our revolution could, at one go and so radically, overcome the limitations and backward provincialism of our national past. Soviet Russia has become not only the refuge of the Communist International; she is the living expression of its programme and its method.

By the unknown ways in which human personality is shaped, ways as yet unrevealed by science, Lenin absorbed from the national environment all he needed to perform the greatest revolutionary act in history. Precisely because in Lenin the socialist revolution, for long elaborated theoretically on an international scale, found for the first time its national realization, he became, in the most direct and most immediate sense, the leader of the international world proletariat.

Such is Lenin today, the day of his fiftieth birthday.

10
The Philistine and the Revolutionary

IN ONE of the many anthologies on Lenin I found an
essay by the English writer H. G. Wells under the title
The Dreamer in the Kremlin.[1] The editors of the volume
remark in the preface that "even such progressive people
as Wells had not understood the meaning of the proletarian
revolution which occurred in Russia."

This, it would seem, was not a sufficient reason for includ-
ing Wells' essay in a volume devoted to the leader of that
revolution. But I do not want to be quarrelsome; in any case
I personally have read not without interest Wells' few pages.
This, however, as will be seen later, has not been due to the
author.

I vividly remember Wells' visit in Moscow. This was
during the cold and hungry winter of 1920–21. There was
in the air an anxious presentiment of the difficulties which
awaited us in the spring. Starving Moscow lay buried in
thick snow. The economic policy was on the eve of a sharp
change. I remember very well the impression which the talk
with Wells made on Lenin: "What a petty-bourgeois! What
a Philistine!" he kept on repeating, raising both his arms,
laughing and sighing in a way characteristic of him when
he felt inwardly ashamed for another man. "Oh, what a
Philistine!" he repeated, recalling the conversation.

We were both waiting for the opening of a session of the

---

[1] See *The Sunday Express*, November 28th, 1920. (Translator's note.)

Politbureau, and in fact Lenin said nothing more about Wells, except what I have just quoted. But this was quite enough. I admit, I have read little of Wells, and I have never met him. But I could well imagine the personality of this English drawing-room socialist, one of the Fabians, a novelist, and the author of fantastic and utopian stories, who had journeyed to Moscow to take a look at the communist experiment. Lenin's exclamations, and quite especially their tone, completed and enlivened the picture.

Now, Wells' essay, which providence in its mysterious ways introduced into a Lenin anthology, not only evoked in my memory Lenin's exclamation, but filled it with living content. Although there is hardly a trace of Lenin in Wells' essay about him, there is in it the whole of Wells himself clearly seen as the back of one's hand.

Let us start from the beginning, from the first complaint made by Wells: poor man, do you know it took him quite some time and some effort to get an appointment with Lenin and this was "tedious and irritating" to him. Why should it have been? Had Lenin invited Wells there? Did he promise to see him? Perhaps Lenin had too much time on his hands? On the contrary, during these difficult days every minute of Lenin's time was taken up; it was not easy for him to carve out one hour in which to receive Wells. This should have been plain even to a foreigner. The trouble was that Wells, as an illustrious foreigner, and, for all his 'socialism' a rather conservative Englishman of imperialist habits, was absolutely convinced that in fact he was by his visit conferring a great honour on this barbarian country and its leader. His whole article, from first to last, oozes this quite groundless conviction.

The characterization of Lenin begins, as one might have expected, from a great discovery. You see, Lenin "is not a writer". Who, in fact, should know this better than Wells, a professional man of letters? "The shrill little pamphlets and papers issued from Moscow in his name, full of misconceptions of the labour psychology of the West . . . display hardly anything of the real Lenin mentality. . . ." The honourable gentleman does not know, of course, that Lenin is the author of a whole series of fundamental works on the agrarian question, on economic theory, on sociology and philosophy. Wells knew only the "shrill little pamphlets"; he also remarked that they were issued "in his name", hinting perhaps that they were written by other people. The real "Lenin mentality" reveals itself not in the dozens of volumes which he had written, but in the hour-long conversation into which the eminent visitor from Great Britain so generously deigned to enter.

One would have expected Wells to give at least an interesting description of Lenin's physiognomy. For a single well-observed, well-rendered feature we would have been ready to forgive him all his Fabian trivialities. But there is nothing of the kind in the essay.

"Lenin has a pleasant, quick-changing brownish (!) face with a lively smile. . ." Lenin "is not very like the photographs you see of him. . ." ". . . he gesticulated a little with his hands during our conversation. . ." Wells did not go beyond the banalities of a commonplace reporter, who has to fill a column of his capitalist paper. In addition Wells discovered that Lenin's head resembled the "domed and slightly one-sided cranium" of Arthur Balfour, and that, generally speaking, Lenin is a "little man: his feet scarcely touch the ground as he sits on the edge of his chair." As far as Arthur Balfour's skull is concerned, we can say nothing about this worthy object and we are ready to believe that it is domed. But all the rest! What indecent trash! Lenin had a reddish-blond complexion and one could not by any means describe him as "brownish". He was of medium height, or a little below that; but that he looked a "little man", whose feet hardly reached the floor might have been only the impression of a Wells who arrived feeling like a civilized Gulliver on a journey to the land of northern communist Lilliputians. Wells also noticed that Lenin, whenever there was a pause in the conversation, was "screwing up one eye";

this habit, explains the shrewd writer, "is due perhaps to some defect in focusing." We know this gesture of Lenin's well. It was always there when Lenin had before him a stranger, with whom he had nothing in common: covering his eyes, he used to throw a rapid glance through his fingers and the "defect in focusing" consisted in no more than that he saw through his interlocutor, saw his self-satisfied vanity, his narrow-mindedness, his 'civilized' conceit and his 'civilized' ignorance. Long afterwards, remembering the occasion, Lenin would shake his head: "What a Philistine! What an awful petit-bourgeois!"

Comrade Rothstein was present during the talk and Wells *en passant* made the discovery that this fact was "characteristic for the present condition of Russian affairs." Rothstein, you see, controls Lenin on behalf of the Commissariat of Foreign Affairs in view of Lenin's extreme frankness and his "dreamer's imprudence". What can one say about such a priceless observation? Wells went to the Kremlin, his mind stuffed with all the rubbishy information purveyed by the international bourgeoisie and with his penetrating eye— without any "defect of focusing"—found in Lenin's office the confirmation of what he had earlier fished out of the pages of *The Times* or from some other source of respectable and genteel gossip.

But what then was the conversation about?

Here Wells conveys to us some hopeless platitudes which only show what a pitiful and hollow echo Lenin's thought evokes in some other heads whose one-sidedness incidentally we have no reason to question.

Wells turned up "expecting to struggle with a doctrinaire Marxist", but in fact he "found nothing of the sort". This should not surprise us. We have already learned that "the real Lenin mentality" has been revealed not during the more than thirty years of his political and literary activity, but in his conversation with the citizen from England. "I had been told that Lenin lectured people; he certainly did not do so on this occasion." How, indeed, to lecture a 'gentleman'[2] so full of self-importance? That Lenin liked to lecture people or to teach them was quite untrue. It was true that one could learn a good deal from a conversation with him. But this happened only when Lenin was of the opinion that his interlocutor was able to learn something. In such cases Lenin spared no time and no effort. After two or three minutes in the company of the wonderful Gulliver who by a lucky chance found himself in the office of the "little man", Lenin must have become firmly convinced that the inscription at the entry to Dante's hell "Abandon all hope!" was quite appropriate in this situation.

The conversation touched upon the problem of big cities. Precisely in Russia, as Wells himself said, a remarkable idea occurred to him, namely, that the outlook of a city is determined by the trade in the shops and in the market places. He shared this revelation with Lenin. Lenin "admitted" that under communism cities might become much smaller. Wells "pointed out" to Lenin that the renovation of cities and towns would constitute a gigantic task and that quite a few of the enormous buildings of Petersburg would retain their significance only as historical monuments. Lenin agreed with this original platitude. "I think it warmed his heart," added Wells, "to find someone who understood a necessary consequence of collectivism that many even of his own people fail to grasp."

Well, this gives you the measure of Wells' level of thinking. He treats as proof of his extraordinary perspicacity the discovery that under a communist regime the existing huge urban concentrations will disappear and that our present monsters of capitalist architecture will preserve their significance as historic monuments only (unless they will be granted the honour of being demolished). Of course, how would poor communists ("the tiresome class-war fanatics") arrive at such discoveries, which, by the way, have a long time ago been described in a popular addendum to the old programme

---

[2] The English word is used in the text.

of the German Social Democratic Party. We shall not mention that all this was quite familiar to the classical utopians of socialism.

Now you will understand, I hope, why Wells did not at all notice that famous laughter of Lenin about which he had been told so much. Lenin was in no mood to laugh. I even fear that he might have been a victim of quite the opposite temptation. But his versatile and clever hand, as usual, rendered him a service by concealing just in time an unkind yawn from a visitor preoccupied with his own person.

As you have learned, Lenin did not lecture Wells—for reasons which seem to us quite obvious. In return, however, Wells persisted in giving Lenin advice. He kept on impressing upon Lenin the completely new idea that for the success of socialism it is necessary to change not only the material side of life but also "the mentality of a whole people." He drew Lenin's attention to the fact that "The Russians are by habit and tradition traders and individualists"; he also explained to him that communism "was pressing too hard and too fast, and destroying before it was ready to rebuild", and so on, and so forth, all in the same spirit. "And that", relates Wells, "brought us to our essential difference—the difference of the collectivist and Marxist." Under 'evolutionary collectivism' one should understand a brew of the Fabians which consists of liberalism, philanthropy, a stingy social legislation together with Sunday meditations about a brighter future. Wells himself thus formulates the essence of 'evolutionary collectivism': "I believe that through a vast sustained educational campaign the existing capitalist system could be civilized into a Collectivist world system." Wells does not make it clear, however, who is going to introduce this "vast sustained educational campaign" and who will be subjected to it: are we to suppose that English 'milords' with 'domed' heads will exercise it over the English proletariat, or, on the contrary, that the English proletariat will subject 'milords'' heads to this education. Oh, no, anything but the latter. For what purpose do we have in this world the educated Fabians, the intellectuals, with their altruistic imagination, the gentlemen and the ladies, the Messrs Wells and Mesdames Snowdens, if not that they should, by a planned and prolonged process of sharing what they themselves carry concealed in their own heads, civilize capitalist society and transform it into a collectivist one, with such a sensible and happy gradualness that even the British monarchy will not notice this transformation?

All this Wells went on expounding to Lenin and Lenin sat listening. "For me," Wells graciously remarked, "it was very refreshing" to talk to "this amazing little man." And for Lenin? Oh, long suffering Ilyich! He certainly had quite a few expressive and racy Russian words on his tongue. He did not utter them aloud nor did he translate them into English, not only because his English vocabulary would not stretch that far, but also because he was much too polite for this. But he could not limit himself to a polite silence alone.

"He [Lenin] had to argue . . ." relates Wells, "that modern capitalism is incurably predatory, wasteful and un-teachable." Lenin quoted facts and figures published, *inter alia* in the new book of Chiozza Money,[3] and showed how capitalism destroyed the English shipyards, how it prevented a sensible exploitation of coal resources, and so on. Lenin knew the language of facts and figures. "I had, I will con-fess," Mr Wells unexpectedly concluded, "a very uphill argument." What did this mean? Wasn't this the beginning of a capitulation of the evolutionary collectivism before the logic of Marxism? No, no. "Abandon all hope."

This admission, which on first sight, seems unexpected, is not at all fortuitous, but forms an integral part of the typically Fabian evolutionary and didactic system. It was, in fact, addressed to the English capitalists, bankers, peers, and their ministers. Wells was telling them: you see, you behave so stupidly, so greedily, so selfishly, that you make it ex-

[3] Leo Chiozza Money, *The Triumph of Nationalization*, Cassell, 1920. (Translator's note.)

tremely difficult for me to defend the principles of my evolutionary collectivism in the discussions with the dreamer in the Kremlin. Listen to reason, take part in the Fabians' Sunday ritual ablutions, civilize yourself, march on to the road of progress.

Wells' melancholy admission was not the beginning of a critical revision of his views, but a continuation of that educative work of the same capitalist society, which after the imperialist war and the Versailles Treaty, has so much improved, so much moralized and fabianized itself.

Not without condescending sympathy, Wells remarks that Lenin "has an unlimited confidence in his work." With this statement we shall not quarrel. Indeed, Lenin had faith enough in the justice of his cause. What is true is true. This faith was also, incidentally, the source of the patience with which Lenin entered into conversations, during these harsh months of the blockade, with any foreigner who could serve as a contact, albeit indirectly, between Russia and the West. So Lenin met Wells. He talked a quite different language with English workers who used to visit him. With them he entered into a lively exchange; he taught them and he learned from them. With Wells the intercourse could not have anything but a strained, diplomatic character. "Our . . . argumentation ended indecisively," sums up the author. In other words, the match between evolutionary collectivism and Marxism this time ended in a draw. Wells returned to Great Britain, Lenin remained in the Kremlin. Wells wrote up his pompous 'correspondence' for his bourgeois public, and Lenin, shaking his head, kept on repeating: "What a petty-bourgeois! Aye, aye, what a Philistine!"

One may ask why and for what purpose I have given so much attention to an insignificant article by H. G. Wells, four years after its publication. The fact that the article was included in one of the anthologies brought out in connection with Lenin's death is not a valid reason. Nor is it a sufficient justification to say that I wrote these lines in Sukhum, where

I was undergoing medical treatment. But I had more serious considerations too.

Just now in England Wells' party is in power. At the head of the party we see the enlightened representatives of evolutionary collectivism. It seemed to me—perhaps not quite unreasonably—that Wells' words devoted to Lenin may perhaps better than anything else reveal to us the spirit of the leaders of the English Labour Party. After all, Wells was by no means the worst of them.

How terribly these people lag behind, pressed down by the leaden weight of their bourgeois prejudices. Their pride, which is nothing else but a time-worn reflex of their historical role in the past, prevents them from penetrating, as they should, the minds of other nations, from examining new ideological phenomena, new historical processes which all pass them by. Routine-ridden, narrow-minded empiricists, with blinkers of their bourgeois public opinion over their eyes, these gentlemen carry with them all over the world their own prejudices; they have a peculiar talent for noticing nothing around them—except themselves. Lenin had lived in various countries of Europe, had learned foreign languages, read, studied, listened, pondered matters deeply, compared, generalized. At the head of a great revolutionary country, he never missed an opportunity to inform himself, attentively and conscientiously, to inquire, to learn. He never ceased to follow the events of the entire world. He read and spoke German, French, and English fluently, and he could read Italian too. In the last years of his life, overloaded with work, stealthily, during the Politbureau's meetings, he studied a Czechoslovak grammar in order to have a more direct contact with the working movement of that country. Sometimes we used to 'catch him out', and, embarrassed, he would laugh and try to excuse himself. Beside him Wells was the embodiment of those pseudo-educated, narrow-minded bourgeois who look without seeing, who do not want to learn anything because they feel so comfortable behind their barrier of inherited prejudices. Then you have

Mr MacDonald, a more solid and gloomy variety of the same type, reassuring public opinion in England: We have fought against Moscow and we have won.

Have *they* won? They are indeed poor 'little men' even if they have grown tall in size. Even now, after all that has happened, they still have no inkling of what the future has in store for them. Liberal and conservative businessmen easily manipulate these pedantic 'evolutionary' socialists now in power, deliberately preparing not only the downfall of their government but their political debacle as well. At the same time, however, only unknowingly, they prepare the path to power for English Marxists. Yes, precisely for the Marxists, for those "tiresome class-war fanatics". The English social revolution too will proceed according to the laws defined by Marx.

Wells, with his peculiar humour so much like a stodgy English pudding, once threatened to cut off Marx's 'doctrinaire' head of hair and his beard, to anglicize him, to make him more respectable and to 'fabianize' him. But nothing came of this project, and nothing will ever come of it. Marx will remain Marx, just as Lenin will remain Lenin, even after subjection to Wells' blunt razor-blade for more than a full tiresome hour. We dare to venture a forecast that in the not too distant future in London, perhaps in Trafalgar Square, there will appear, next to each other, two monuments in bronze: one of Karl Marx and the other of Vladimir Lenin. And English workers will say to their children: "What a good thing it was, that the little men of the Labour Party did not manage either to cut the hair or to shave the beards of these two giants."

Awaiting this day, which I hope to be alive to see, I shut my eyes for a second and I see clearly Lenin's figure in the same chair in which Wells saw him, and I hear—after Wells' visit or perhaps a day later—the slightly mournful yet good-natured voice: "What a petty bourgeois! What a Philistine!"

April 6th 1924

11
The True and the False[1]
(On Lenin's portrait by Gorky)

"IT IS difficult to draw his portrait," says Gorky of Lenin. This is correct. Gorky's writings about Lenin are very poor. The fabric of his description seems to be woven of various kinds of yarn. Now and again there passes a thin thread more brilliant than the others and one feels the artistic sensitivity behind it. But there are many more threads of banal psychological analysis, and one notices all too frequently the very petty bourgeois moralist. As a whole, the tissue is not too beautiful. But as Gorky was the weaver, his *oeuvre* will be examined for a long time to come. This is why it should be discussed. Perhaps we shall find an opportunity better to understand, or better to notice, certain characteristics, large or small, of Lenin's personality.

Gorky is right when he says that Lenin is the extraordinary and perfect embodiment of a tense will striving towards the goal. This *tension towards the goal* is Lenin's essential characteristic. I have said this before and shall come back to it again. But, when a little further, Gorky treats Lenin as "one of the righteous", this sounds false and is in bad taste. The expression "the righteous", borrowed from the Church, from the language of religious sects with the odour of Lent and the oil of holy icons, does not accord with Lenin at all. He was a great man, a magnificent giant, and nothing human was alien to him. During one Congress of the Soviets there came to the rostrum a fairly well-known representative

[1] This essay is translated from *Pravda*, of October 7th, 1924, where it was first published. It was not included in the Russian edition of the book. (Translator's note.)

of a religious sect, a communist christian (or something of the kind), very clever and cunning. He straightway intoned a psalm praising Lenin as The Father, the giver of all good things. I remember that Vladimir Ilyich, sitting at the table with other members of the Presidium, lifted his head, as if a little frightened, then turned slightly towards us and whispered, very angrily, to those nearest to him:

"What are all these obscenities?"

The word 'obscenity' escaped him quite unexpectedly, as if unwittingly, and yet it was the right word. I was controlling my laughter; I was savouring Lenin's incomparable and spontaneous description of the praises sung by the very christian speaker. Well, Gorky's expression "the righteous" has something in common with the 'Father-the-giver-of-all-good-things' of the pious man. It is, if you allow me to say so, an 'obscenity' on a small scale.

What came later was even worse:

"For me Lenin is a legendary hero, a man who tore from his breast a flaming heart to lift it like a torch and to light men's way..."

Brrrr. How horrid. It reminds one of the old Izerghill (I think this was the name of the old witch so popular in the days of our youth) and the story of her relations with the gypsy Danko. In that story, if I am not mistaken, there is also a heart which changes into a torch. Or is it in some opera...? Yes, I mean an *opera*: with decor imitating a southern landscape, with the lighting of fireworks and a gypsy band. Yet in Lenin's personality there is nothing which could possibly suggest an opera and even less of anything that can bring to mind the romanticism of itinerant gypsies. Lenin is a man from Simbirsk, from 'Piter',[2] of Moscow, of the world—a hard realist, a professional revolutionary: there could be nothing in common between Danko, the hero of the fable, and Lenin who disparaged romanticism, theatrical pretence and bohemian revolutionism. Those who are in

---

[2] Abbreviation of Petersburg.

need of revolutionary models borrowed from gypsy tales should rather look for them in the history of Social Revolutionaries.

Then, three lines lower down, Gorky adds:

"Lenin was as simple and as straightforward as all that he was saying."

If it were so, then why should we imagine him tearing out a flaming heart from his breast? In such a gesture there would be no simplicity, no sincerity. . . But these two words "simple" and "straightforward" are not chosen with great felicity; they are much too commonplace and plain. One uses these terms to describe an honest young lad, a brave soldier, who babbles 'plain truth' whatever it might be. These terms do not fit Lenin at all, no matter how we understand them.

Certainly, he had the simplicity of a genius in the way he took decisions, in the conclusions he used to reach, in his methods, in his activity: he knew how to reject, to push aside, to disregard all that had no real importance, that was only incidental or superficial; he knew how to reach the heart of the matter, how to reduce a problem to its essentials.

But all this does not mean that he was just "simple" and "straightforward". Even less does it mean that his thought followed a "straight line", as Gorky maintains somewhere else—a most regrettable expression, worthy indeed of a petit-bourgeois and a Menshevik.

In connection with this I suddenly remembered a definition given by the young writer Babel who spoke about "the complex curve of Lenin's straight line." Contrary to the first impression these words make, and in spite of the antinomy and the over-elaborate subtlety of the juxtaposition, the definition is nevertheless correct. In any case, it is immeasurably better than the 'straightforwardness' used by Gorky. A man who is just "simple" and "straightforward" marches straight towards his goal. Lenin marched and led towards one and the same goal by an indirect and often very roundabout way. Last but not least, the two adjectives put together—"simple and straightforward"—give not the slightest idea of Lenin's inimitable slyness, his quick and brilliant ingenuity, the passion of a virtuoso with which he delighted in tripping the adversary and seeing him fall, or in ensnaring him into a trap.

We have already mentioned Lenin's singleness of purpose, his tense striving towards the goal. On this characteristic we should dwell a little longer. One critic, believing he had discovered a deep truth, started explaining to me that Lenin distinguished himself not only by this tenseness of will with which he pursued his goal, but also by his dexterity as a tactician. The same critic reproached me that in the portrait I had given of Lenin, stressing the rock-like hardness of the great man, I had failed to emphasize his suppleness.

The critic who had thus taken me to task, though he differed from Gorky, did not understand the relative weight and meaning of words either. Indeed, it is extremely difficult to make people aware that "the tenseness in striving towards the goal" does not necessarily imply marching "in a straight line." And what would Lenin's suppleness be worth without this tenseness which did not flag even for a moment?

In this world one finds as much political suppleness as one wants: bourgeois parliamentarism is an excellent school in which politicians are constantly trained in flexibility, where they constantly learn how to bend the backbone. If Lenin had very often mocked "the straight line of the doctrinaires," he had just as often showed contempt for those who are too supple, too flexible, those who bow down not necessarily, and not always, before their bourgeois masters, not indeed in order to derive some advantage—but, say, before the pressure of public opinion, or in the face of a difficult situation—just taking the line of least resistance.

The very essence of Lenin, all his most inward worth, consists precisely in this: that always and everywhere he was pursuing his unique goal, the importance of which he felt so deeply that it became as if organically his, it became part of himself—he was at one with the aim he was pursuing and there was no means of drawing a line between his person and his purpose. He could not view people, books, events, otherwise than through the prism of this unique purpose of his existence.

It is impossible to sum up a man in one word. To say that he was 'great' or that he was a 'genius' really means nothing. But if I were to attempt briefly to define what sort of man Lenin was, I would stress that his whole being was geared to one great purpose. He possessed *the tenseness of striving towards* his goal.

Gorky remarks on Lenin's captivating laughter: "The laughter of a man who, perceiving so clearly the whole weight of human stupidity and the acrobatic tricks of reason, was able to delight in the childlike artlessness of those of simple hearts." Expressed somewhat laboriously, this is substantially correct. Lenin laughed at stupid and malicious people who tried to be clever; and he laughed with the tolerance justified by his enormous superiority. Some of those nearest to Lenin laughed with him though not always for the same reasons. . . But the laughter of the masses always accorded well with his. He liked those of 'simple hearts' (to use the evangelical expression). Gorky describes how, in Capri, Lenin learned the art of angling from Italian fishermen. These good people explained to him: tag fast when the rod makes 'drin, drin'. As soon as Lenin, feeling the pull of the hook, caught his first fish, he exclaimed with *childish joy*, with the *enthusiasm of a real beginner*:

"Oho, drin, drin!"

This is excellent. Here is a truly living bit of Lenin. This passion, this rapture, this tense will to achieve his aim, to 'tag fast' and get his prey—"oho, drin, drin! That's it! there it is!"

How far all this is from the Righteous, Lent, the Giver-of-all-good-things which we have quoted. This is the true Lenin, a living part of him. When Lenin, catching a fish, shouts his enthusiasm, we guess his lively delight in nature, in everything that is near nature, in children, in animals, in music. His powerful thinking mechanism was not far removed from what is *outside* thought, outside conscious brain work—it was not far removed from the primitive and the unspoken. Precisely what cannot be put into words is expressed by "drin, drin". For giving us this memorable detail, we should be prepared to forgive Gorky a quarter of all the banalities spread over his whole essay. It will be seen later on that we cannot, however, forgive him more than a quarter...

"He caressed children with great tenderness," Gorky tells us, "stroking them lightly with extreme delicacy." This is also well said; it shows us the man's affection which goes together with the respect, physical and moral, for the child's personality. One would notice the same in Lenin's handshake—vigorous and yet gentle.

Lenin's attitude to animals I remember best from the following episode:

We were holding a meeting in the mountain village of Zimmerwald and our commission was charged with preparing a manifesto. We were sitting at a round table in the open air. Not far away under the tap stood a large vat full of water. Just before our meeting (which was arranged rather early in the morning) a few delegates washed themselves under that tap. I saw Fritz Platten plunging head first and up to his waist into the water as if he were out to drown himself, to the great consternation of the other participants in the conference.

The work of the commission took a distressing turn. There were disagreements on various points, but mainly between Lenin and the majority. At that moment two splendid dogs came into the garden. I do not know what kind of dogs they were—at that time I knew nothing of the breed of dogs. They must have belonged to the owner of the place, because they started playing peacefully on the sand in the morning sunshine. Vladimir Ilyich suddenly got up and left the table. Half-kneeling, he started laughing and tickling, first one dog then the other, under their ears, along their bellies, lightly, delicately (to use Gorky's expression). There was spontaneity in Lenin's gesture: one is tempted to say that he behaved like a little urchin, so carefree, so boyish was his laughter. He glanced at our commission as if he wanted to invite the comrades to take part in this lovely diversion. It seemed to me that people looked with some astonishment: everybody was still preoccupied by the serious debate. Lenin went on stroking the animals, but in a less ebullient manner. He then returned to the table and refused to sign the proposed text of the manifesto. The discussion began anew with fresh violence. It occurs to me now that it was quite possible that Lenin was in need of 'diversion' in order to weigh in his mind the arguments for and against the decision to sign. But he did not act with any premeditation; his subconscious and his conscious thought worked in complete harmony.

Gorky admired in Lenin "this youthful ardour which went into all he did." This ardour was disciplined and dominated by an iron will, just as a mountain stream is kept in check by its granite banks. Gorky did not seem to notice this, but his remark is nevertheless true: There was in Lenin this "youthful ardour" and also "the unique spiritual courage of those who are profoundly, unshakably sure of their purpose". This, again, is well said and shrewdly observed. But, in other instances, the fusty and flabby language, the odour of sanctity or the "asceticism" (!) or "monkish heroism" (!!) do not at all accord with the youthful ardour—they just mix like fire and water. "Sanctity" and "asceticism" are characteristic of a man who devotes himself to the service of a 'superior' spiritual principle, of a man who goes against his leanings and has to tame his personal passions. His asceticism is calculated because he expects to be rewarded for it. Lenin in his historical task was fulfilling himself completely and absolutely.

"The omniscient eyes of a great sly fox"—this is not bad, though formulated somewhat coarsely. But how can one

have such eyes and at the same time be "simple", "straightforward" and, above all, have that aura of "sanctity"?

"He was fun-loving," Gorky tells us further, "and he
laughed with all his body, truly overwhelmed with gaiety,
he sometimes laughed literally to tears." This was true and
was known to all that came into contact with him. At some
gatherings at which there were not many people, Lenin
would sometimes have a fit of laughter, and that happened
not only when things went well, but even during hard and
difficult moments. He tried to control himself as long as he
could, but finally he would burst out with a peal of laughter
which infected all the others. He forced himself to be quiet,
to conceal his merriment, sometimes even bending down
under the table, anxious not to disorganize the meeting.
Such hilarity used to take hold of him especially when he
was tired. I remember the familiar gesture: moving his arm
up and down, he was as if driving away the temptation. All
in vain. He devised only one method of controlling himself:
he would fix his gaze on his watch with the greatest concentration, carefully avoiding other people's eyes and he would
put on an extremely severe expression—in this way, with an
affected stiffness, he would maintain the calmness befitting a
chairman. In such cases it was the comrades' point of honour
to 'catch the eye of the speaker' and to provoke, by some
jest, a relapse into hilarity. If they succeeded, the chairman
was furious both with the culprit and with himself.

Of course, such diversions did not occur very often; when
they did, it was usually towards the end of the session, after
four or five hours of intense work, when everybody was
exhausted. Normally, Ilyich used to conduct debates with
the utmost strictness, and it was due to this method that we
were able to dispose of innumerable problems during a single
session.

"He had his particular expressive way of murmuring
'hm, hm'," continues Gorky, "and he could invest this 'hm,
hm' with an infinite gamut of meaning from biting irony
to doubt and circumspection; and often this 'hm, hm'

expressed a sharp sense of humour, noticed and understood only by the discerning and wise, who knew the devilish absurdities of existence." This is true and very correct. The "hm, hm" played indeed an important role in Lenin's conversations with those who were closest to him, and also in his controversies. He pronounced his "hm, hm" very clearly, each sound separately: "H-m, h-m," and, as Gorky rightly says, with an infinite variety of nuances. It did constitute a kind of signalling code which he used to express a great wealth of different feelings and moods. On paper "hm, hm" means nothing; in a personal talk it is endowed with a multitude of shades and acquires value by the tone of voice, by the movement of the head, by the flicker of the eyebrows, and by the eloquent gesture of the hands.

Gorky describes also Lenin's favourite posture:

"He would throw his head backwards, then to the side over the shoulder, would stick his thumbs into the armholes of his waistcoat under the armpits. There was in this posture something astonishingly funny and charming, one would say a victorious cock—and at such moments he was all radiant."

All this is quite well said, except for that "victorious cock" which in no way fits Lenin's image. But the posture is excellently depicted. Alas! Let's read further:

"The great child of this sinful world, the wonderful man who felt the need to sacrifice himself, to offer himself as the victim of hostility and hatred in order to bring about the labour of love and beauty. . ." Please, Alexei Maximovich, have pity. . . . ". . . child of this sinful world . . ." oh! the pharisaic odour of this sentence! Often Lenin's manner was strikingly engaging, sometimes malicious, but there was nothing hypocritical about him. ". . . to offer himself as victim. . ." No, this is false, untrue, unbearably false! It jars on one's ears like a screw scraping on glass.

Lenin did not sacrifice himself. On the contrary, he lived a full life, a wonderfully abundant life, developing, expanding his whole personality, serving a cause which he himself freely chose. And his labour was not that of "love and beauty"—such high flown and well worn words mean nothing. Only capital letters are missing here: Love and Beauty. No, Lenin's task, which he took upon himself, was that of awakening and uniting the oppressed, so that they could free themselves from oppression—and this was the cause of ninety-nine per cent of humanity.

Gorky tells us about Lenin's attentiveness towards his comrades, about his solicitude for their health, and so on. And adds: "In this watchfulness I never detected the kind of selfish preoccupation which an intelligent boss shows towards his honest and efficient workers."

Well, here Gorky was completely wrong, because he completely missed one of Lenin's main characteristics. The personal attentiveness which Lenin showed his comrades was never devoid of the solicitude of a good boss who always bears in mind the work to be done. Of course, one cannot speak about 'selfishness', because there was nothing selfish in his preoccupation. Lenin's personal attentiveness towards his comrades was dictated by his devotion to the cause— precisely to the same cause for which the comrades themselves gathered around him; about this there can be no doubt. This attention which Lenin gave to them both as his co-workers and as individuals, in no way detracts from his humanity. It only testifies once again to his singleness of purpose, to the tenseness with which his whole personality was geared to the achievement of his aim.

Gorky, who did not notice this, was certainly unable to understand why Lenin reacted as he did to Gorky's innumerable intercessions in favour of people who had 'suffered' in the revolution. As we all know, there were many victims of the revolution; there were also very many appeals in their favour which Gorky addressed directly to Lenin. Some of these were indeed ridiculous. It is enough to recall his fantastically insistent intervention in defence of the Social Revolutionaries during the famous trial in Moscow.

Gorky relates: "I do not remember a single case in which Lenin had refused my request. If it happened that Lenin's directives were not followed, this was no doubt not his fault, but the result of those accursed 'technical defects' which were always so numerous in our governmental machinery. There was also plain ill-will on the part of some people who simply did not want to help, and did not care to save lives. . . ."

We must admit that this statement by Gorky shocked us more than anything else. What does all this suggest? Does it mean that Lenin, as the leader of the party and the head of the state, persecuted mercilessly all the enemies of the revolution, but that Gorky's intervention was a sufficient reason for him to relent? That there was "not a single case" in which Lenin refused the writer's request? That the fate of men was settled by a friendly chat with Lenin? This assertion would have been quite incomprehensible, if it were not for Gorky's remark that his intercessions were not always effective. For this he blames the "technical defects" of the governmental machinery. Was this really so? Was Lenin really so helpless as to be unable to overcome these "defects" in a simple matter of releasing a prisoner, or sparing somebody punishment? This is extremely dubious. Would it not be more logical to assume that Lenin, having glanced at the petition and at the petitioner with his "omniscient eyes of a great sly fox," just avoided entering into a discussion with Gorky, entrusting to the Soviet machinery, with all its defects, real and imaginary, the question of acting in the best interests of the revolution? Indeed, Lenin was not all that "simple" and all that "straightforward" when he had to defend himself against petty bourgeois sentimentality. True, Lenin's respect for human personality was enormous, but it was also subordinated to his respect and solicitude for mankind as a whole, which in our epoch means in the first instance the world proletariat. If Vladimir Ilyich had been unable to subordinate the particular to the general, he might have indeed been one of the Righteous who offered himself as a martyr in the cause of Love and Beauty, but he would not by any means have been Lenin the leader of the Bolshevik Party and of the October Revolution.

It is in the light of what I have just said that one should understand the "extraordinary stubbornness" with which, according to Gorky, Lenin for over a year insisted that Gorky should go abroad for medical treatment. "In Europe, in a good sanatorium you will undergo a cure and you will be able to do three times as much work as here. Aye, aye! Go abroad, take care of your health, please, go. Don't be obstinate."

The warm sympathy which Lenin had for Gorky, for the man as well as for the writer, was unmistakable and widely known. No doubt, Gorky's poor health worried Vladimir Ilyich. Nonetheless, in his stubborn insistence that Gorky should go abroad there was also a political motive. In Russia, during these difficult years, Gorky was getting hopelessly confused and might have gone tragically astray; abroad, looking at capitalism and its civilization, he was more likely to find his bearings, to recover the mood which once in the past had made him "spit in the face" of bourgeois France. Incidentally, it would have been unnecessary for him to repeat this quite meaningless 'demonstration'. But the feeling behind this instinctive gesture was much more productive than the soul-saving intercessions on behalf of those workers in the field of 'culture' whose sufferings were due only to the fact that they, poor people, did not manage in time to tighten the hangman's noose around the neck of the proletarian revolution.

Of course, Lenin took great care of Gorky. Of course, he sincerely desired that Gorky should recover his health, that he should live and work. But he needed a 'straightened out' Gorky. That was why he stubbornly insisted on sending him abroad to get again a whiff of capitalist culture. Even if one knew nothing about the background to this relationship, one could easily have inferred Lenin's motives from Gorky himself. Lenin acted indeed like an "intelligent boss" who never and in no circumstances loses sight of the good of the cause entrusted to him by history.

It was not as a revolutionary writer but as a petty bourgeois moralizer that Gorky sketched the portrait of Lenin. As a result the figure of Vladimir Ilyich, so exceptional in its unity, breaks up on Gorky's canvas.

But things look even worse when the writer discusses politics in the proper sense of the word. Here in every sentence there is either misunderstanding or plain falsehood. "A man of extraordinary willpower, he was in all other respects a typical Russian intellectual."

Lenin—a "typical Russian intellectual"? Isn't this a monstrous joke? Lenin—a *typical* intellectual? But this does not seem enough for Gorky. According to him, Lenin "possessed in the highest degree the quality so characteristic for the élite of Russian intelligentsia: self-denial which sometimes led to self-torment, to self-mutilation. . . ." Just listen to this! The fat is in the fire! A few pages before Gorky expatiates profusely on the subject of Lenin's heroism and that "modest asceticism with which one meets not rarely in Russia among the honest revolutionary intellectuals who sincerely believe in the possibility of justice on earth", and so on, and so forth. This phrase is so disgustingly false that it is physically impossible to go on quoting it. "Honest Russian intellectual who believes in justice on earth." Whichever way you look at this, you can only imagine a petty radical official from the provinces who had gulped down the historical letters of Lavrov[3] or their counterfeit version produced belatedly by Chernov.

This reminds me of one of those translators of Marx who once described him in print as "the great Jeremiah of popular

---

[3] P. L. Lavrov (1823–1900), mathematician, philosopher, and revolutionary writer. Took part in the Paris Commune, was a friend of Marx and Engels. His *Historical Letters*, a philosophical work, published in book form under the pseudonym P. Mirtov, had a tremendous influence on Russian intelligentsia. He was one of the main ideologues of the Populists. (Translator's note.)

affliction." Twenty-five years ago, in the small town of Nizhnyi Ilinsk, I laughed heartily at this Karl Marx of the provinces. And now it comes to pass that Lenin too does not escape a similar fate. It was no other than Gorky, who had seen Lenin, who knew him well—he was among his friends —who sometimes worked with him—this same Gorky now presents this giant of revolutionary thought not only as a pious ascetic, but even worse, as a typical Russian intellectual. This really borders on calumny, all the more detestable as it is made in good faith, with good intentions, and almost with enthusiasm. Of course, Vladimir Ilyich was steeped in the tradition of the radical revolutionary intelligentsia, but he transcended this tradition and only then became—Lenin. A "typical" Russian intellectual is extremely limited in his outlook; Lenin's outlook and intellect knew no limits.

If it be true to say that Lenin was nurtured by the century-old tradition of Russian radical intelligentsia, it is even more true that he was the product of the elemental force and pressure which the peasant mass has for long centuries exercised on the country. In Lenin there lived the Russian muzhik, with his hatred for the landlord, with his calculating spirit, his clever husbandry and his shrewdness. But Lenin transcended all that was petty and narrow in the muzhik by the soaring flight of his thought and his most powerful will. Finally, Lenin became the embodiment—and this was stronger in him than anything else—of the spirit of the young Russian proletariat; and not to see this, but to see only the intellectual in him, is to see nothing. What constituted Lenin's genius? It consisted precisely in this: that through him the young Russian proletariat liberated itself from the conditions shackling its development and reached towards the heights of historic universality. Lenin's personality, deeply rooted in the soil of Russia, burst forth, grew organically, expanded into creative and genuine internationalism. Lenin's genius consisted, first of all, in transcending all confines.

Gorky defines rather neatly one of Lenin's main characteristics by calling it "fighting optimism". He also adds: "In this there was nothing Russian. . ."

Well, how is it then? "The typical intellectual", the provincial "ascetic"—was not all this most Russian? Wouldn't that make, say, a good chap from Tambov? How is it then that with all these non-Russian features like an iron will and a fighting optimism, Lenin was at the same time the "typical Russian intellectual"? Isn't Gorky casting a grave aspersion on Russians generally? The talent to lead lice on a leash is unquestionably Russian, but thanks to dialectics it is not everlasting and immutable. The social revolutionary policy, which reached its apogee in the Kerensky regime, was the highest expression of this folklore art of leading lice on a leash. But, let me tell you, Alexei Maximovich, that the October revolution would have been impossible if well before that date a new fire had not been kindled in Russian men and women.

Ours was the epoch not only of Russian history's turning-point, but also that at which the whole national spirit underwent a transformation. You maintained, Alexei Maximovich, that Lenin's essential features were not 'Russian'. . . Allow me to ask you: Is the Bolshevik Party a Russian phenomenon or perhaps . . . a Dutch phenomenon? What would you say about those proletarians engaged in clandestine work, about the fighters and partisans, about the men from the Urals, hard as rock itself, about the Red Commissars who day and night kept their finger on the triggers of their revolvers, who today are at the head of industry, of plants and factories, and who tomorrow would be ready to lay down their lives for the liberation of the Chinese coolies? What breed of people, what species, what segment of humanity are they? Were they not made of Russian clay?

The Russia of the twentieth century (and of the earlier one as well) is no longer the old provincial land of past epochs. It is a new, an internationalist Russia with steel in its character. The Bolshevik Party is the best part of that new Russia, and Lenin its supreme builder and guide.

Here we are stepping into the thick of a great confusion. Gorky declares himself, not without belated coquetry, "a doubting Marxist" who does not believe in the intelligence of the masses in general and the intelligence of the peasantry in particular. He maintains that the masses have to be ruled "from outside", from above.

"I know", Gorky goes on, "that by voicing such ideas I am exposing myself again to the scorn of politicians. I also know that the most intelligent and the most honest among them will mock me insincerely, from their, so to speak, sense of duty."

I do not know who those "intelligent" and "honest" politicians are who share Gorky's scepticism about the masses. But their scepticism seems to me rather flat. That the masses need guidance ("from outside"), that much, we think, Lenin had guessed. Perhaps Gorky has heard that precisely because of that need Lenin spent his whole conscious life in building up a special organization, namely the Bolshevik Party. Lenin never encouraged any blind faith in the reason of the masses, but he had even more contempt for the arrogance and conceit of the intellectual who reproached the masses that they were not made in his excellent image and after his likeness. Lenin was aware that the intelligence of the masses had to be adapted to the objective development of circumstances. The party was to facilitate this process. History testifies that it achieved its task.

Gorky, as he says himself, parted with the communists because of a divergence of views on the role of the intellectuals. He maintains that the better ones among the old Bolsheviks brought up hundreds of workers precisely "in the spirit of social heroism and high intellectuality" (!!). In simpler words and more exactly it means, that Gorky accepted Bolshevism in its laboratory stage, when it was forming and educating its first intellectual and working-class cadres. He feels near enough to the Bolshevik of 1903–1905. But the man of 1917, mature and formed, who with a sure hand put into practice what fifteen years before one could only perceive—such a Bolshevik is a stranger whom Gorky views with hostility.

Gorky himself, with his constant aspirations towards higher culture and higher intelligence, managed somehow to stop half-way. He is neither a layman nor a Pope of culture, but some sort of a psalmist. Hence his haughty attitude, his contempt for the intelligence of the masses and also for Marxism, though Marxism in contrast with subjectivism, bases itself not on faith in the reason of the masses, but on the logic of the materialistic processes which, in the final analysis, determine and form that 'reason'.

But that road is not easy and on the way quite a lot of crockery gets broken (some of it created by 'culture'). This is what Gorky cannot endure. According to him, one should be satisfied with just admiring all these lovely ceramics, all the pottery, the pots and pans; one should not break them.

Gorky wants to find an affinity with Lenin, and so he consoles himself thus: "Vladimir Ilyich also, probably more than once, had to hold down his soul by its wings," that means to do violence to himself: implacable when he had to crush resistance, Lenin was thus a prey to interior conflicts because he had to restrain his love of man, his love of culture. In such a way Gorky presents Lenin as the heir to the respectable malaise, the "sick conscience", that split personality, which once upon a time was the bane of the old radical intelligentsia. But all this is untrue. Lenin was all of a piece: 'a piece' of very high quality, of complex structure, but with all its components held perfectly together and constituting one solid entity.

The truth is that Lenin often avoided busybodies, mediators, and petitioners: "Let X talk to him," he used to say with an evasive smile, "I may prove too good." Yes, he sometimes feared to prove "too good", because he knew the craftiness of the foe and the sanctimonious foolishness of mediators and considered in advance that no amount of caution was too much. He preferred to deal with the invisible enemy than to be distracted by accidental circumstances where he might show himself "too good". But even in this there was his calm political calculation and by no means that "sickly conscience", which always goes together with lack of will, lachrymosity and the maudlin nature of the "typical Russian intellectual".

But this is not yet all. Gorky, as he himself tells us, reproached Lenin with a "simplified understanding of the drama of existence" (hm, hm !!); such poor understanding, he says, "puts culture in mortal danger" (hm, hm!). During the critical days at the end of 1917 and the beginning of 1918, when in Moscow shots were fired at the Kremlin, when sailors were throwing cigarette butts at the *Gobelins* (such things did happen, but not as often as the bourgeoisie alleged), when soldiers, as it was said, were cutting up the canvases of Rembrandt to make themselves trousers (extremely uncomfortable and not very practical)—this was the kind of complaint with which whimpering representatives of "high intellectuality" were coming to Gorky. At that time Gorky quite lost his balance and became a real mourner of culture. Horror and vandalism! The Bolsheviks are going to break all the historical vases and pots, flower-pots, kitchen-pots, and chamber-pots!

And Lenin would answer: "We shall break as many as we have to, and if we break too many, the fault will lie not with us but with those intellectuals who defend untenable positions." Wasn't this proof of a narrow mind? Don't you see—Oh, Lord, have mercy—that Lenin oversimplified "the drama of existence"?

It is not worth while even to quibble about all this. Lenin's whole life was devoted not to bemoaning the complexity of existence, but to changing it. For this existence has to be viewed in its entirety, with its main elements and trends of further development clearly seen; all else is of little significance. Precisely because Lenin had this great talent of creatively going straight into the heart of the matter, he considered "the drama of existence" in a business-like manner: we shall break this, we have to demolish that, and temporarily we have to prop up something else.

Lenin noted all that was honest, all that was individual. He noticed all particulars and every detail. If he "simplified" or, in other words, rejected all that was inessential, it was not because he did not see it, but because he knew to perfection the relative value and proportion of things.

All this brings to my mind a worker by the name of Vorontsov, who just after October was detailed to guard Lenin's person and to help him. As we were preparing to evacuate Petrograd, Vorontsov said to me gravely:

"If it so happens that *they* take Petrograd, *they* might find quite a lot that's useful. . . We should put dynamite under the whole city and blow it all up."

"Wouldn't you regret Petrograd, comrade Vorontsov?" I asked admiring his boldness.

"What is there to be regretted? When we are back, we shall build something much better."

I have not invented that brief dialogue, nor have I stylized it. Such as it was, it remained engraved on my memory. That was the correct attitude towards culture. No lamentation and no wails of woe. Culture is the product of human hands. True culture lies not in the decorated pots of history, but in the good organization of the labour of human hands and minds. If on the way to achieve such an organization there are obstacles, they have to be swept aside. And if, in the process, we are forced to destroy some values of the past, then let us destroy them, but without sentimental tears. We shall return to build anew and to build incomparably better. That was how Lenin, and with him millions of men and women, felt and thought. This was right and just. From this revolutionaries of all countries can learn a great deal.

Kislovodsk, September 28th 1924.

12
Children on Lenin[1]

"In Russia
There was only one
Vladimir Ilyich Lenin."
(From a child's poem.)

A DELIGHTFUL and quite exceptional little book has
appeared recently: a collection of children's writings
about the life and death of Lenin.[2] The authors, whose
ages range between nine and fourteen years—there is even
one girl of five—write about the great old man.

Of course, many simply reproduce what they had heard
from the grown-ups. But here and there among the, so to
speak, stereotyped texts appears an unexpected breath of such
freshness that the most familiar phrases come to life again,
as if revived by a spring shower; one also finds the inimitable, colourful spontaneity of creative childhood. The poems
are, as usual, rather weaker than the prose. Rules of poetry-
writing are too restrictive and hamper directness of expression. But even among the poems some are astonishing.

"There is no such spot," writes one child, "where they
would not know the father of the proletariat, the strong,
the courageous, the brave, the resourceful, the wise Lenin."
This list, in which the finest qualities are enumerated one
after the other, expresses completely children's ideas about
Lenin: he possesses all the virtues that make a man absolutely perfect.

---

[1] This essay is not included in the first Russian edition of Trotsky's
book. Here it is translated from *Pravda* of October 8th, 1924. (Translator's note.)

[2] *Ilyich*, ed. Anna Grinberg, *Novaya Moskva*, 1924.

"When he was imprisoned with his comrades, he always sang: 'Forward, comrades, forward!'" This remark shows a deep conviction that in prison one should not become dejected, one should keep up the spirit of one's mates, and so "the brave, resourceful" Vladimir Ilyich goes on singing "Forward, comrades, forward." The others sing with him, but, of course, he leads the chorus. Who else could lead it? The same child continues: "Before, when Lenin was still alive, I was sure that if nothing came of the German revolution and if the capitalist countries marched on Russia, then Ilyich, although already ill, would get up from his bed and would fight to the last drop of blood. That was how I imagined Ilyich would sacrifice himself." One can see here how political ideas, drawn from newspaper articles (the defeat of the German revolution, capitalist attack on the Soviet Union) are linked with the direct, spontaneous yet convincing and unspoilt childish image: when the revolution is in trouble, the ill and aged Ilyich rises from his bed and fights "to the last drop of his blood." Only death prevented him from "sacrificing himself" on the final barricade. The author ends his piece thus: "Now that Lenin is no more one should not be afraid." Once this boy grows up, he will surely find a place for himself on the Leninist barricades.

There is also in the book a biography of Lenin in which the whole story of Lenin's family is told: we learn about his father, about Alexander who was shot, and about his sister Maria, now the 'editress' of *Pravda*. Exiled to Siberia, Lenin liked "playing games and often went racing on skates or something else, and when he ran he would strain all his forces to win the race and not to be beaten by the others." As you see, this image of Lenin is quite different from that so often presented to us: Lenin, the morose saint, who wherever he appears looks immediately for a dark humid room where he can shut himself up. What disgusting bigotry! No, the children's Lenin—and the real one—liked running races and "strained all his forces so as not to be beaten by others."

Here I cannot refrain from recalling an amusing episode. Together with Vladimir Ilyich we introduced a 'rule' that anybody coming more than ten minutes late to a session should pay a fine. I remember that just after emerging from one meeting we had to attend another taking place at the far end of the Kremlin, for which we had to cross a very long esplanade. Ilyich decided to go home for a while. I phoned him: "Vladimir Ilyich, you risk paying a fine, you have only two to three minutes left before the session begins."

"It's all right," answered Ilyich with a little giggle, the sense of which I understood only later. I walked downstairs and reaching the courtyard I kept on looking back to see whether Vladimir Ilyich was anywhere to be seen. Suddenly, at the far end, about a hundred paces in front of me, a familiar figure whizzed past and vanished round the corner of the Cavalry Building. "Was this Lenin? Impossible. It cannot be."

Two minutes later I reached the conference room. Whom did I see? Lenin. Still slightly short of breath, he met me with a joyful "Hallo, it is you who are one minute late!" and he burst out in triumphant laughter.

"I must admit," I explained to the other comrades, "I did not expect... True, it seemed to me that someone resembling Vladimir Ilyich flew by towards the Cavalry Building, but I could not imagine that the Chairman of the Council of People's Commissars would—in the full view of all—rush like a hurricane across the esplanade of the Kremlin." Ilyich was chuckling; he was triumphant. All this happened exactly as in that child's biography: Vladimir Ilyich summoned all his strength and would not let anybody overtake him.

But let us go back to the main story.

After the Siberian exile—emigration; after that—the revolution, and then the man had to go into hiding to avoid being caught by Kerensky. The children forget nothing. "Even from his hiding-place comrade Lenin was directing the revolution and was sending out letters. And when the

Soviet was in session, Lenin *presided over it from his hut* as a delegate present at the meeting." Could this have been put better? Here is Lenin hidden in a shack and, as Chairman, presiding over the assembly of the national deputies. This was indeed how things happened. However, the vagaries of the climate made such a method of governing rather inconvenient. "It started raining," goes on the young biographer, "and it became cold in the hut." The tactic had to be modified and some other way of directing the revolution had to be found. Of course, Ilyich found it: not for nothing was he "strong, courageous, brave, resourceful, wise." He went for a time to Finland. And this is what later happened: "Comrade Ilyich had no more patience to wait: he returned to Piter [Petersburg] and there organized the October insurrection. Power was taken over by workers and peasants." This was true. It is even true that Lenin had "no more patience to wait".

One of the young authors describes his meetings with Lenin. The boy was with his father in the Kremlin, on the esplanade. Suddenly: Ilyich. Having shaken hands with the father, Lenin stretched his hand towards the boy. "I got so excited that I dropped my basket. Before I had time to pick it up, Vladimir Ilyich had already bent down and then he shook my hand which I put out to take the basket from him. Then he put his hand on my head and asked my father:

"'Is it this one or your older one who is a Bolshevik?'

"'This one. The older one is a Whiteguardist. He fights against the young scamps of Comrade Trotsky, and he is also too lazy to learn...'

"'Well, never mind! The time will come when he will also be a Bolshevik', says Vladimir Ilyich.

"He spoke quickly and smiled all the time."

This dialogue is reproduced with admirable exactitude: the words, the turn of phrase, and the gestures were really Lenin's. Indeed, "he spoke quickly and smiled all the time." This faithfulness in reproduction of the conversation is due to the receptiveness and freshness of memory of the author.

To listen to Lenin was to him like the first sight of a tremendous fire or a tremendous waterfall.

Another little boy listened to Lenin who spoke on the Red Square to the workers urging them to unite and form one big family: "I stood in the car next to the driver and I looked at Lenin. *I liked him.*" The author does not bother to explain why. For him it is absolutely clear that people are divided into those that one likes and those one does not. "*I liked him*", that is all. Full stop.

Yet another boy describes how he saw Lenin. He had a more difficult job. "On the square there was an enormous crowd and everybody shouted 'Ilyich'. I wanted to climb onto something, but there was nothing. I was pushed about. I even started to cry because I so much wanted to see Lenin. In the end I grabbed the back of a workman, I put my foot into his pocket and then I hoisted myself onto his shoulders as if on horseback. I thought he would shake me off straightway and give me a kick too. To my surprise the workman, saying that I was a rascal, told me to hold fast to his neck. I found myself two heads above everybody else and I saw Ilyich."

Well, you will admit that not everybody would find a similar way. In any case, you would probably be put off by the mere idea of *your* foot in a *stranger*'s pocket. But our Alexander of Macedon from the Presnia suburb is not put off by such a trifle. And because it had occurred to him to put *his* foot into the pocket of a stranger and because in addition the stranger did not slap him, but allowed him to remain on his observation post (not, however, without calling him a rascal), we have received a remarkable eyewitness description of Lenin as speaker:

"He got up on the platform. He was wearing a dark, I think a black suit, a shirt with a turn-down collar and a tie, and a cap on his head. He pulled a white handkerchief from his pocket and wiped his bald head. I do not remember what he said. I was really paying more attention to how he was speaking. *Sometimes he kept bending down quite low from the platform*, stretching his arms in front of him; he had his handkerchief in his hand and often wiped his forehead. He often smiled. I was watching his face, his nose, his lips, and his small beard. His speech was often interrupted by clapping and shouting. And so I also shouted."

Indeed, how could one refrain from shouting? What exemplary precision in the portrayal. Lenin wipes his forehead and his bald head with a white handkerchief, now and again bends down stretching his arms towards the crowd. How alive Lenin is in this picture. What he actually said, our author does not remember. This does not really matter, as the speech anyhow was taken down by stenographers. The lively figure of Lenin, however, remains engraved on the eager memory of a little man sitting on a stranger's back. "I was watching his face, his nose, his lips, and his small beard"—he will remember this all his life. On his way home he kept on repeating: Lenin, Lenin, Lenin. The boy was carrying away a load of wonderful impressions. He stopped to look at every photograph of Lenin on the street. . . Lenin died without knowing that sometimes in order to watch him one had to put one's foot in a stranger's pocket. How wholeheartedly he would have laughed at this 'Bolshevik' manner of solving a difficult tactical problem. . .

Here is another detail from the biography of the leader: "Lenin liked fishing. On a hot day he would take his fishing-rod and would sit down on the bank of a river and *all the time he would think how to improve the life of the workers and peasants.*" What imagination! The hook is thrown into the water; the man sits on the bank and waits until the fish takes the bait (which does not happen often); in the meantime he looks at the water and thinks hard, very hard, how to improve the lot of workers and peasants. That's what Lenin did! And because of this the fishing is seen in a meaningful light:

> There was only one
> Vladimir Ilyich Lenin. . . .

In races he ran fast; he did not like the tsar and the capitalists; he was fishing and thinking hard how to improve the life of workers and peasants. In prison he was singing aloud "Forward, comrades, forward"; he directed the revolution from a hut and was loudly urging the workers to unite and was wiping his bald head with a handkerchief; he knew everything, he was wise, and he taught. But he died. The strong and courageous father of the proletariat died. And this extraordinary, mysterious and terrible news which came from above, from the grown-ups, shattered children's world.

On January 22nd the teacher at school was speaking about Lenin's death: "And the teacher, much affected, talked haltingly and we, all of us, listened intently and in the end we could not stand it any longer and hot tears were flowing down our cheeks. Then the children could not listen any more, because they were all crying and so we all got up and sang the Funeral March."

The boys and girls who on January 22nd 1924 were shedding hot tears and singing the Funeral March will relate all this to their children and their grandchildren. And so the story will be passed on from generation to generation.

The news of Lenin's death reaches a worker's family: "My mother sat at the table and had a knife in her hand. When she heard about the death of Ilyich, she dropped the knife and she started to cry although she did not know her great leader." How convincing is the 'dropped knife' and how well the child remarks that the mother cried "*although she did not know her great leader*".

A little girl returned home after having listened to a talk on Lenin and she "related every detail to her family: that Ilyich did not like luxuries, that he liked children, that he liked to work a lot." Everything has its place: the work is put last and "luxuries" first, children just in the middle. And adult would probably see things in a different order. It was only after having heard the girl's story that the mother gave credence to the news and "got very alarmed." Then the girl together with her Komsomol sister sat down to sew black ties.

A small boy from a Children's Home relates how Oscar Andreevich (evidently quite familiar to the author though unknown to us) was hanging out a black flag as a sign of mourning. "And there goes a fat woman and pushing us aside says: 'Out of the way. . . . Haven't you seen how rags are being put out?' And I said *very, very quietly*: 'Stupid woman, she doesn't understand a thing!'" John Huss remarked of an old ignorant woman: Oh, holy simplicity!— different formula, different epoch, and different the age of the man who pronounced the words, but the spirit was the same.

"At the beginning of that day we were cheerful, but when we learned—we became very sad." How expressive is this brevity. Then they go to see the dead: "The coffin, a red cushion. He was there, very pale. I looked at him all the time." The little John Huss woke up next morning and he very much wanted to have a portrait of Lenin. That is what he says: "In the morning I got up and *I greatly needed* Lenin's portrait." Straightway he drew a picture and to give vent to his feelings, he placed a small red star and the letters USSR and RSFSR on Lenin's forehead. In this way everybody would know whose picture it was.

"Dear great leader," writes a little girl to the dead Lenin, "I thought that you will recover, but unexpectedly death came. I so much regret it and it makes me so sad that I shall not see you any more." With these words she ends her brief letter which will be read by everyone except its addressee.

> "Echoes in the hills resound:
> Ilyich is no more
> But an answer can be found:
> Do not lose courage."

Well, the rhymes are rather poor, but how much they express: the death of Ilyich has moved even the hills and the author hears the echo in Moscow. However, this sombre news must be met by a call of bravery and courage. Not for nothing did Lenin teach his comrades in prison to sing: "Forward, comrades, forward".

Lenin is dead. He is carried to the House of the Trade Unions in Moscow where his body is laid out.

> "They looked at him, the young and the old,
>   The peasant and the worker—and yet *he did not*
>   *know.*
> Once he gave us the Soviets.
> Now he lay in his coffin
> Quite still.

"And yet he did not know . . ." the author became suddenly aware that Lenin who knew everything, yet now did not know that people looked at him: Such is the meaning of death.

And now the funeral: "Around the House of the Trade Unions many people were waiting for him. The citizens of the town did not expect to meet him in such a manner. They thought: here will come the chief ruler in a golden carriage and all will be glittering. But the workers recognized in him their own, their well-beloved Ilyich." On the one hand a political distinction between the "citizen of the town" and the worker: on the other, the truly childish images: "the chief ruler", "the golden carriage", all "glittering".

Another description of the funeral:

> "One speaker, and another, and the third, and the
>   fourth.
> From different countries, from different states
>   they came.
> Now the last words are already said
> And *Lenin without fear* descends into the tomb."

The small heart is rent at the idea that Ilyich, that Lenin has to descend into the grave, but here comes a clear and consoling thought: ". . . without fear. . ." How could it be otherwise: Fearless all his life and now he died without fear. This is no mysticism, but an artistic image of the leader.

Endlessly, endlessly, people are passing in front of the red coffin, adults and children—the future authors of reminiscences:

"And behind us I could hear somebody sobbing,
   Somebody's piercing scream.
We are passing and passing with our hearts
      throbbing,
Seing his yellowing face never enough seen."

This is well said; especially good is the last line.

Here is another story, realistically descriptive, less lyrical, and without political accents:

"We joined one of the queues on the Mokhovaya Street. In front of us we could see only heads, and above them banners. The crowd was silent. Then a pedlar passes and shouts: 'Hot pies, hot pies'. A woman said: 'Go away, this is no time for pies!' The queue moves slowly and there are already many people behind us. Everybody feels the cold. The frost pinches our feet, our hands, and faces." Did Shakespeare learn from children the gift of combining the tragic with the trivial, the great with the petty? Under a bleak sky millions of people are burying their leader. Amid all this: "Hot pies, hot pies!" and the rebuff: "Go away, this is no time for pies". Finally, our author reached the hall: "On a raised platform the red coffin and he in the coffin. One would give one's life to save him. No, that is impossible. The illness took what belonged to it. His face is yellowish, as if made of wax. The nose sharper, the expression severe. The beard exactly as in pictures, and the arms in repose as if he were alive. He is dressed in a green French[3] and on his breast the Order of the Red Banner." How observant the eye of the author and with what precision he

---

[3] A kind of military jacket common in Russia since the war.

conveys his impressions. Through the sober, factual description bursts out the sentiment in all its freshness: "One would give one's life to save him." A little further the narrative is again interrupted by an exclamation: "Oh, too soon, Ilyich, too soon." This sounds like a reproach but it comes from the bottom of the heart. The most cogent remark ends the piece:

"People descend and go out, but their faces are not as they were before: waiting to be let into the hall, they were expectant and a little impatient; now, with their heads bent, they all look down—everybody tries to fix the image of Vladimir Ilyich in their memory for ever."

This essay shows such power of observation and is so well done that one might suspect an adult had written it. And yet an adult would not write in this manner; I, at least, have not come across anything of that kind.

"He was lying in the red coffin," writes a very young author (or rather authoress—a *pendant* to the 'editress'), "and there was music and his beard was just the same as it used to be in his pictures. When I saw this, I started crying."

No, one could not hold back the tears when one saw the beard, the same beard which he had when he was alive. In children's recollections Lenin's beard becomes a very important element. It seems to symbolize maturity, manliness, and the fighting spirit. Lenin had a small beard but it was full of meaning because it was *his*. Also the beard was "exactly like in the pictures," the pictures were therefore true; therefore everything else was true. The little girl goes on to describe how all by herself she made a badge to pin on to her frock. The quotation would take us too far. But anyone seriously thinking of producing a Lenin badge with no money to buy one, should read this book. He will find in it all the required information. . .

One more poem, a dramatic one, about the death of Lenin:

"When they were carrying you to the grave
Millions of people were walking behind you,
They were walking with flags and banners.

People were crying, canons were firing,
Factory sirens were whining.
The whole world knew that you were dead."

This was how we buried the leader. The plants and the factories were shaken by the sound of sirens and canons. The flags and the banners and the canons proclaimed the greatness of the deceased. Millions were crying over your grave. "The whole world knew. . ." Thus we were burying you, Ilyich. Thus we were parting from you.

Perhaps the best is the funeral dirge sung by a five-year-old girl in a kindergarten:

"You died, Ilyich.
A bird flew in
And warmed itself in the sun.
You died, Ilyich!
And you were buried.
And your clothes died.
You died, Ilyich!
And you were left all alone,
Poor, poor Ilyich.
You were good.
I shall give you my room
And I love you.
You'll come back into the light again
And we shall be able to touch you."

The little girl's thoughts are wandering: it is so difficult to concentrate and to collect one's thoughts. A bird flows in and warms itself. But something grave has happened: Ilyich died and was buried and his clothes died with him, because they live and die. "You were left all alone, poor, poor Ilyich!" But is all this so final? Perhaps if I gave you my room you will return into the light again and we shall be able to touch you. Does not life mean that one can touch and be touched? This was what a little girl sang about Lenin. Nobody has composed a better song. Great poets will come much later; they will read what the children wrote in this book; they will ponder deeply, and they will sing:

"In Russia
There was only one
Vladimir Ilyich Lenin."

Kislovodsk, September 30th 1924.

13
Lenin Wounded[1]

COMRADES, the brotherly greetings with which I am received are for me a sign that in these difficult hours and days all of us, like brothers, feel a profound need to draw closer to each other, to our Soviet institutions, to tighten our ranks under the communist banner. In these hours and days of anxiety when the standard-bearer of our proletariat, and, we can say, of the world proletariat, is struggling with the terrible spectre of death, we feel closer to each other than in the hours of victory. . .

The news of the attempt at Lenin's life reached me and some other comrades in Svyazhsk, on the Kazan front. Blows were falling fast, from the right, from the left, and straight on our heads. But this latest blow hit us at the back, it was delivered from behind. Treachery opened up another front, the most painful, and at the present time the most alarming: the one on which Vladimir Ilyich struggles against death.

I firmly believe together with all of you, that from all the battles we might still have to fight, we shall soon emerge victorious. Whatever partial defeats we may still suffer, none will be as terrible, as tragic for the working class of Russia and of the whole world, as the fatal issue of the battle going on for the life of our leader.

One can imagine quite easily with what violent hatred all the enemies of the working class look upon Lenin and will be looking upon him. It is as if nature were producing its

[1] Speech at the session of the All-Union Central Executive Committee, September 2nd, 1918.

very best by embodying in one man both the essence of revolutionary thought and the indomitable energy of the proletariat. Such a man is Vladimir Ilyich.

The gallery of those who led the revolutionary fighters is rich and varied. Like other comrades who have been engaged in revolutionary work for nearly three decades, I have met in many countries various types of workers' leaders, of revolutionary representatives of the working class. But only Comrade Lenin is the man truly created for our epoch of blood and iron.

We have left behind the period of the so-called peaceful development of bourgeois society, when conflicts of interests were mounting only gradually, when Europe was experiencing a time of what was called armed peace, and blood was flowing only in the colonies where rapacious capital was tormenting the most backward peoples. Europe enjoyed peace under the regime of capitalist militarism. It was also the formative period for the most notable leaders of the European labour movement who then were coming to the fore. Among them was the great and brilliant August Bebel. But in him was mirrored the epoch of the gradual and slow development of the working class; he combined great courage and iron energy with extreme prudence in action; he kept probing the situation and his was the strategy of waiting and preparation. He expressed the process of gradual, molecular gathering of forces; his thought proceeded step by step in the same manner in which the German working class in the period of reaction was itself moving forward step by step, freeing itself from obscurantism and prejudice. His moral stature grew, expanded, acquired strength and magnitude, but always on the same basis of waiting and preparation. Such were the ideas and the methods of August Bebel, the most valuable figure of that epoch which has already passed into the eternity of history.

Ours is a different epoch—the time when old accumulated contradictions reached an explosive stage, breaking through the surface of bourgeois society when the very foundations of world capitalism were shaken by the terrible slaughter of European nations. In our epoch all the various class antagonisms were laid bare and the masses were forced to face the horrible reality of the death of millions for the sake of the profit and riches of a handful. And for such an epoch Western Europe forgot, or was unable, to provide a leader. This was not just an accident: all leaders who on the eve of war enjoyed the greatest trust of the European working class represented the yesterdays of that class and not the actuality of the present day...

When the new epoch dawned, the old chiefs were unable to keep pace with that age of terrible convulsions and bloody battles. History wished, not fortuitously, to create in Russia a figure carved in rock, a figure which accorded well with all the ferocity and greatness of the times. No, it was no accident.

1847 produced in backward Germany the figure of Karl Marx, the greatest fighter and thinker who charted history's new roads. Yes, Germany was then a backward country, but at the same time Germany's intelligentsia was going through a phase of revolutionary development; its most eminent representatives enriched by all the science it had acquired, broke with bourgeois society, and choosing the side of revolutionary proletariat, elaborated a programme for the labour movement and for the working class a theory of its development.

What Marx had predicted in his time, our epoch has been called upon to fulfil. For this new leaders were needed, leaders who would carry in them the flame of the new age in which the working class, having risen to the height of its historic task, clearly saw the great divide that had to be crossed if mankind was to be saved, if it was not to be allowed to putrefy like carrion dropped by the roadside of history.

For this new age Russian history created a new leader.

All that was best in the old revolutionary intellectuals of earlier times: their spirit of self-denial, their audacity, their hatred of oppression—all this was concentrated in the figure of this man who, already in his youth, broke irrevocably with the intelligentsia because it was too strongly tied to the bourgeoisie; this man absorbed completely the spirit and the just cause of the working class. Supported by Russia's young revolutionary proletariat, utilizing the rich experience of a world-wide workers' movement, transforming its ideology into a lever for action, he has risen to his full stature on the political horizon. This is Lenin, the greatest man of our revolutionary epoch. (*Applause*)

I know, and you know as well as I do, comrades, that the fate of the working class does not depend on individual personalities; but this does not mean that the individual personality is of no importance in the development of the working class. The individual cannot remould the working class after his own image and likeness, nor can he, at will, show the proletariat this or that road to follow, but he can help in the accomplishment of the necessary tasks and speed up the attainment of the goal. Critics reproached Karl Marx that he expected the revolution to come about much sooner than in reality it took place. The answer, and a very valid one, to this reproach was that Marx stood on the top of a high mountain and from there the distance seemed to him much shorter than it was.

Vladimir Ilyich was often criticized by many comrades, and by myself among them, for seemingly not paying attention to secondary matters and certain side issues. I should think that in times of 'normal' slow development this might have been a defect in a political leader; but in this lay Comrade Lenin's preeminence as the leader of a new epoch, in which all that is inessential, all that is incidental and secondary recedes into the background, becomes overshadowed, and what remains is only the basic irreconcilable class antagonism in the acute form of civil war. It was Lenin's peculiar gift, which he possessed to the highest degree, that with his intense revolutionary gaze, he could see and point out to others what was most important, most necessary, and most essential. Those comrades who, like myself, were given the chance to observe Lenin's activity and the working of his mind at close quarters, could not help but enthusiastically admire—yes, I repeat, enthusiastically admire —the perspicacity, the acuteness of his thought which rejected all that was external, accidental, superficial, and reached to the heart of the matter and grasped the essential methods of action. The working class learns to value only those leaders who, having opened new paths, go forward with determination even if the proletariat's own prejudices temporarily hinder their progress.

To Lenin's powerful thought is added the power of his will; such thought and such will go into the making of a truly revolutionary leader, courageous, strong in mind and unshaken in determination.

It is our good fortune that in all we say and hear and read in resolutions about Lenin we do not bemoan his loss. And yet we were so near this. . . We are sure that in the battle which goes on there in the Kremlin, life will overcome and that Vladimir Ilyich will soon return to our ranks.

Comrades, I said that Lenin is the embodiment of the courageous thought and revolutionary will of the proletariat. There seems to be a symbol, an international pattern of history in the fact that in these difficult hours when the Russian proletariat, straining all forces, fights on the military fronts against the Czechoslovaks, the White Guards, the mercenaries of England and France, our leader struggles with the wounds inflicted on him by the agents of the same White Guards, the same Czechoslovaks and the same Anglo-French mercenaries. There is here an inner bond and a profound historical symbol. Just as we are all convinced that in this our fight on the Czechoslovak, Anglo-French and White-Guardist front we grow stronger with every day, with every hour that passes (*applause*)—and I speak here as an eye-witness who has returned straight from the scene of military operations—yes, we are growing in strength and we shall be stronger tomorrow than we have been today, and the day after we shall be even stronger—I do not doubt that soon the time will come when we shall be able to tell you that Kazan and Simbirsk, Samara and Ufa, and other towns temporarily occupied by the enemy, are re-joining our Soviet family—in the same way, we firmly hope we shall see the speedy recovery of Comrade Lenin. But even now, at this very moment, the splendid image of our wounded leader, who is out of action for the time being, stands clearly before us. We know that he never left our ranks, because even when mowed down by treacherous bullets, he prods us all to action, he rouses us and urges us to move forward. I have not seen a single comrade, a single honest worker who would, on learning the news about the base attempt on Lenin's life, let his arms fall in dejection. On the contrary, I saw dozens who clenched their fists, whose hands sought their guns; I saw and I heard hundreds who vowed implacable vengeance on the class enemies of the proletariat.

No need to relate to you what were the feelings of the fighters on the front when they learned that Lenin was lying here with two bullets in his body. Nobody could ever say that there was no steel in Lenin's character; now the enemy drove steel right into his flesh. This makes him even more precious to the working class of Russia.

I do not know whether our words and the throbbing of our hearts can be heard at Lenin's bedside, but I have no doubt that he feels it all. I have no doubt that even through his fever he feels that our hearts beat two and three times stronger. Clearer than ever before we are now aware that we are all members of one Soviet communist family. Never yet has the life of any one of us seemed to us so secondary in importance as it does now, at a moment when the life of the greatest man of our times is in mortal peril. Any imbecile can fire at Lenin's head, but to create such a head is a hard task even for nature itself.

Yes, yes, he will soon be up again to think, to build, to fight together with us. On our part we promise our dear leader that as long as in our own heads there still exists some power of thought and hot blood still throbs in our hearts, we shall remain faithful to the banner of the communist revolution. Against the enemies of the working class we shall fight to our last breath, to our last drop of blood. (*Stormy and prolonged applause.*)

14

Lenin Ill[1]

COMRADES, during the year our party, its capacity for clear thinking and the firmness of its will, has been subjected to a new test. This test was all the more severe because it came as a consequence of an event which weighs heavily on the consciousness of all members of the party, of the broad masses of the working population, or, to be more accurate, on the working masses of our country and, to a considerable degree, on the working masses of the whole world. I am speaking of the illness of Vladimir Ilyich. At the beginning of March his condition took a turn for the worse and the Politbureau met in session to consider ways of informing the party and the country about the deterioration in his state. You will, I am sure, all realize the mood of the session, at which we had to issue to the public this first sad and alarming bulletin.

Of course, even in such a moment we had to bear in mind our political responsibilities. Nobody will reproach us with this. We had to think not only of the state of health of Comrade Lenin. True, we were all preoccupied with his physical condition, with his pulse, his heart, his fever; but we also had to think about the reaction which the medical bulletin would have on the political pulse and the political heartbeat of the working class and of our party.

With anxiety, but also with profound faith in the strength of our party, we decided that our comrades and the whole country should be informed at the appearance of the first

---

[1] From a speech at the VIIth conference of the Ukrainian Communist Party, April 5th, 1923.

danger signal. Nobody was in doubt that our enemies would try to exploit the news in order to sow panic among the population, especially in the countryside, to spread all sorts of alarmist rumours, and so on, and so forth. Yet we were all convinced that the party should immediately know how things stood, because to tell the truth amounted to raising the sense of responsibility of each and every member of the party.

Ours is a vast organization embracing half a million people. This is a great community with a great deal of experience, and in this huge mass of comrades Lenin's place is absolutely unique. The whole of history does not know of a single man who could have had such an influence on the destiny not only of one country but on that of the whole of mankind; there is no yardstick, there can be none, to measure the historical importance of Lenin. It is therefore understandable that the fact of his prolonged absence from work and of his serious condition could not but provoke deep anxiety in our political life. Of course, of course, we know that the toiling masses will achieve victory. Don't we have in our song the words: "Nobody will become our saviour ...."; and further: not even "a hero. .." This is true in the final reckoning of history: the working classes finally will conquer, even if there had been no Karl Marx, even if Ulyanov-Lenin had never existed. The working class would by itself have arrived at the ideas which it needed and would have elaborated the methods called for, but all this would have been much delayed, would have been much slower. The circumstance that at two high points in its development, the working class were granted such two figures as that of Marx and of Lenin proved a tremendous advantage to the revolution. Marx was a prophet with the Tables of the Law; Lenin was the executor of the commandments, addressing himself not to the aristocracy of the proletariat as Marx had done, but speaking to the masses, to the people, acquiring new experience in the most difficult conditions, acting, manoeuvring, and coming out victorious.

This year Vladimir Ilyich could only partly share in our practical work. In matters of ideology we have had from him recently a few warnings and directives concerning the question of peasantry, of the state apparatus, and the problem of nationalities. These guidelines will serve us well for quite a few years.

And now we had to announce the deterioration in his physical condition. It was natural that we should have been asking ourselves with deep anxiety how would this news be received by those outside the party: by the Red Army man, by the peasant. In our ruling circle Lenin is the only one who had the confidence of the peasant masses. Apart from everything else, Lenin represents the great moral capital of our Soviet Government in the relations between the working class and the peasantry. Would not the peasants expect— some of us were wondering—that Lenin's policy would undergo a change since he himself was out of action for such a prolonged period? How would the Party react to the news? What effect would the bulletin have on the working classes, on the country?

After the first alarming bulletins were published, the whole party pulled itself together, closed its ranks and improved its morale. Naturally, comrades, the party consists of living human beings, and human beings have their failings and weaknesses; among communists there is a great deal of what is "human, only too human", as the German saying goes. There are among communists factional conflicts, personal conflicts, some serious disagreements and some insignificant ones, and there always will be, because a large party cannot live otherwise. But the moral strength of the party, its political worth is determined by what comes to the surface at the time of a tragic crisis like the present: the discipline, the wish for unity, or, on the contrary, the incidental, the personal, the "human, all too human". I think, comrades, that by now we can already with certainty draw the following conclusion: feeling that it might for a long time be deprived of Lenin's leadership, the Party has become more united than ever, it has rejected all that might endanger the clarity of its thought, the unity of its will and its fighting capacity...

Before I took the train to come here to Kharkov, I had talked to our Moscow Commander Nikolai Ivanovich Muralov, whom many of you know as an old Bolshevik, about the effect the news of Lenin's illness has had on the Red Army men. Muralov said: at first they were all as if struck by thunder, they instinctively recoiled, but then they reflected and began to think more seriously about Lenin and all he represented.

Yes, comrades, the non-party soldier of the Red Army began to wonder in his own way, but in all seriousness, about the role of the individual in history; he began to think about those problems which we, of the older generation learned as schoolboys or students or young workers from books read in prisons, in hard labour camps or in exile where we discussed and argued about the relations between 'the hero' and 'the masses', about subjective and objective factors in a given situation, and so on, and so forth. And now, here, in 1923 our young soldier turned his mind towards all these problems and towards the concrete question of Lenin's role in history; and with the soldiers hundreds of thousands of Russian and Ukrainian and other peasants are posing the same question. What answer do they receive from our political instructors, from our commissars, from our group secretaries? They say: Lenin is a genius; a genius is born no more than once in a century and world history knows only two who have assumed the leadership of the working class, and these two are Marx and Lenin. One cannot create a genius by decree of even the most powerful and most disciplined party, but one can try within the limits of one's possibilities to make up for the absent genius by redoubling our collective efforts. In such a form our political instructors can popularize the theory of relations between the individual and the class among the non-party army men. This is the correct theory.

Lenin is absent from work, therefore we have to redouble our efforts, all together; all of us have with increased vigilance to protect the revolution from any danger that might threaten it; with increased determination we must use every opportunity for constructive work. And we shall do this, every one of us, from the member of the Central Committee to the non-party soldier of the Red Army.

Our labour is very slow, comrades. Although the scale of endeavour is vast, we proceed step by step, and the methods are very 'prosaic': balance sheets and budgeting, taxes in kind and export of grain. All this proceeds tardily and we are constructing the edifice brick by brick. . . Is there not a danger that our party will degenerate into a petty catchpenny? We cannot tolerate this sort of degeneration any more than we can allow, even in the slightest degree, any split within the effective unity of the party. Even if the present state of affairs should be seriously prolonged, it will not, however, last for ever. Perhaps it will not last very long at all.

A revolutionary upheaval on a grand scale, such as the beginning of a revolution in Europe, may come earlier than many of us now expect. One of the strategic lessons which Lenin had taught us has to be particularly firmly kept in mind, namely, what he called *the politics of great turning points*: today on the barricades, and tomorrow in the trough of the Third Duma; today a clarion call to a world revolution, to a world-wide October—and tomorrow negotiations with Kühlmann and Czernin and the signing of the shameful Brest-Litovsk Peace. The circumstances have changed or we assess them differently—we march westwards, on Warsaw. . . . We are forced to revise our view of the situation—and there is the Riga peace treaty which, as you all know, can also be called shameful. . .

Besides—there is stubborn everyday work, brick by brick: economy, cutting down expenses, verification: do we need five telephone operators or would three suffice? And if so, do not employ five, because this will cost the muzhik some additional *poods* of grain which he will have to deliver! Such are the everyday commonplace details of work, but, look! Will not the flame of revolution come from the Ruhr? Will it find us debased, demoralized? No, comrades, we are not degenerating, but we are changing our methods and our procedures, and the revolutionary safeguarding of the party still remains our first and foremost preoccupation. We are learning the job of accountancy and, at the same time, we keep a look-out sharply towards the West and towards the East and events will not catch us napping. By purging and enlarging our proletarian base . . . we are prepared to make a compromise with the peasantry and with the petty bourgeoisie, we are tolerating the NEP-men, but into our party we shall not admit either a petty bourgeois or a NEP-man; if need be, we shall burn them out of the party with sulphuric acid or red hot iron. (*Applause.*)

At the Twelfth Congress, which will be the first Congress since October without Vladimir Ilyich, one of the very few Congresses in the history of our party at which he will not be present, we shall tell ourselves, we shall deeply engrave on our memory the precept: don't get ossified, remember the art of sharp turnings, manoeuvre, but don't become diverted; enter into short-term or even long-term alliances, but do not let your allies infiltrate the party, remain true to yourself, remain the spearhead of the world revolution. And when from the West comes the beating of drums—because it will come—then, although we may be up to our necks in calculations, balance sheets and the NEP, we shall answer at once and without any hesitation: We are revolutionaries from head to foot, we have been and we shall remain revolutionaries to the very end. (*Stormy applause, the whole audience stands up and applauds.*)

15
Lenin is Dead

LENIN is dead. Lenin is no more. Obscure laws by which the work of the blood vessels is ruled have put an end to this life. Medical science proved impotent to achieve what was so passionately demanded by millions of human hearts. Many were those who would have unhesitatingly given their own blood, to the last drop, to revive, to restore the arteries of the great leader, Lenin, Ilyich, the unique, the only one. No miracle happened where science proved helpless. Lenin is no more. These words fall upon our mind as heavily as a giant rock falls into the sea. Can one believe it? Can one make peace with this?

The workers of the whole world will refuse to resign themselves to this fact, for the enemy is still terribly strong, the road is still long and the great task, the greatest in history, is not yet completed. The working classes the world over need Lenin—he is needed as perhaps no other man was ever needed in history.

The second attack of illness, more severe than the first, lasted over ten months. The arterial system, according to the bitter expression of the doctors, kept 'playing up'. What cruel play with Lenin's life! One could expect an improvement, almost a full recovery: but catastrophe was to be expected too. We were all awaiting recovery, and instead, catastrophe came. The brain cells which control the breathing refused to function: the prodigious thought was destroyed.

Now Ilyich is no more. The party is orphaned; and so is the working class. It is this feeling that came before all others at the news of our teacher's, our leader's death.

How shall we go forward? Shall we keep to the road, shall we not go astray? For Lenin, comrades, is no longer with us.

Lenin is no more, but Leninism remains. What was immortal in Lenin—his teaching, his work, his method, his example—lives on in us, in the party which he founded, in the first workers' state he led and guided.

Our hearts are now so overcome with grief because we were all privileged by history which made us Lenin's contemporaries; we worked next to him, we were taught by him. Our party represents Leninism in action; our party, collectively, leads the working masses. In all of us there lives a small part of Lenin, and this is the best part of each one of us.

How shall we go forward? With the torch of Leninism in our hands.

Shall we find the way? With our party's collective mind, with our party's collective will, we shall find the way.

Tomorrow, and the day after, and in a week and in a month we shall still ask: Is Lenin no more? Because his death will for long continue to seem impossible, incredible, a terribly arbitrary deed of nature.

Let that same sharp stab which we feel, which our hearts will feel at the thought that Lenin is no more—let this pain become for each of us a reminder, a warning, a summons: You bear a greater responsibility now. Be worthy of the leader who taught you.

In grief, mourning, and sorrow we shall close our ranks and hearts, close them more firmly for the new battles ahead.

Comrades-brothers, Lenin is no longer with us. Farewell, Ilyich, farewell, our leader.

Tiflis Railway Station.
January 22nd 1924.